THE SCIENCE SPELL BOOK

MAGICAL EXPERIMENTS FOR KIDS

CARA FLORANCE

sourcebooks
eXplore

Text © 2022 by Cara Florance
Cover and internal design © 2022 by Sourcebooks
Cover design by Maryn Arreguín/Sourcebooks
Internal design by Michelle Mayhall/Sourcebooks
Photography © Cara Florance
Illustrations © Cara Florance and Sourcebooks
Illustrations by Cara Florance, Maryn Arreguín/Sourcebooks, and Michelle Mayhall/
Sourcebooks

Published by Sourcebooks eXplore, an imprint of Sourcebooks Kids
P.O. Box 4410, Naperville, Illinois 60567–4410
(630) 961-3900
sourcebookskids.com

Cataloging-in-Publication Data is on file with the Library of Congress.

Source of Production: 1010 Printing Asia Limited, Kwun Tong, Hong Kong, China
Date of Production: August 2023
Run Number: 5034486

Printed and bound in China.
OGP 10 9 8 7 6

CONTENTS

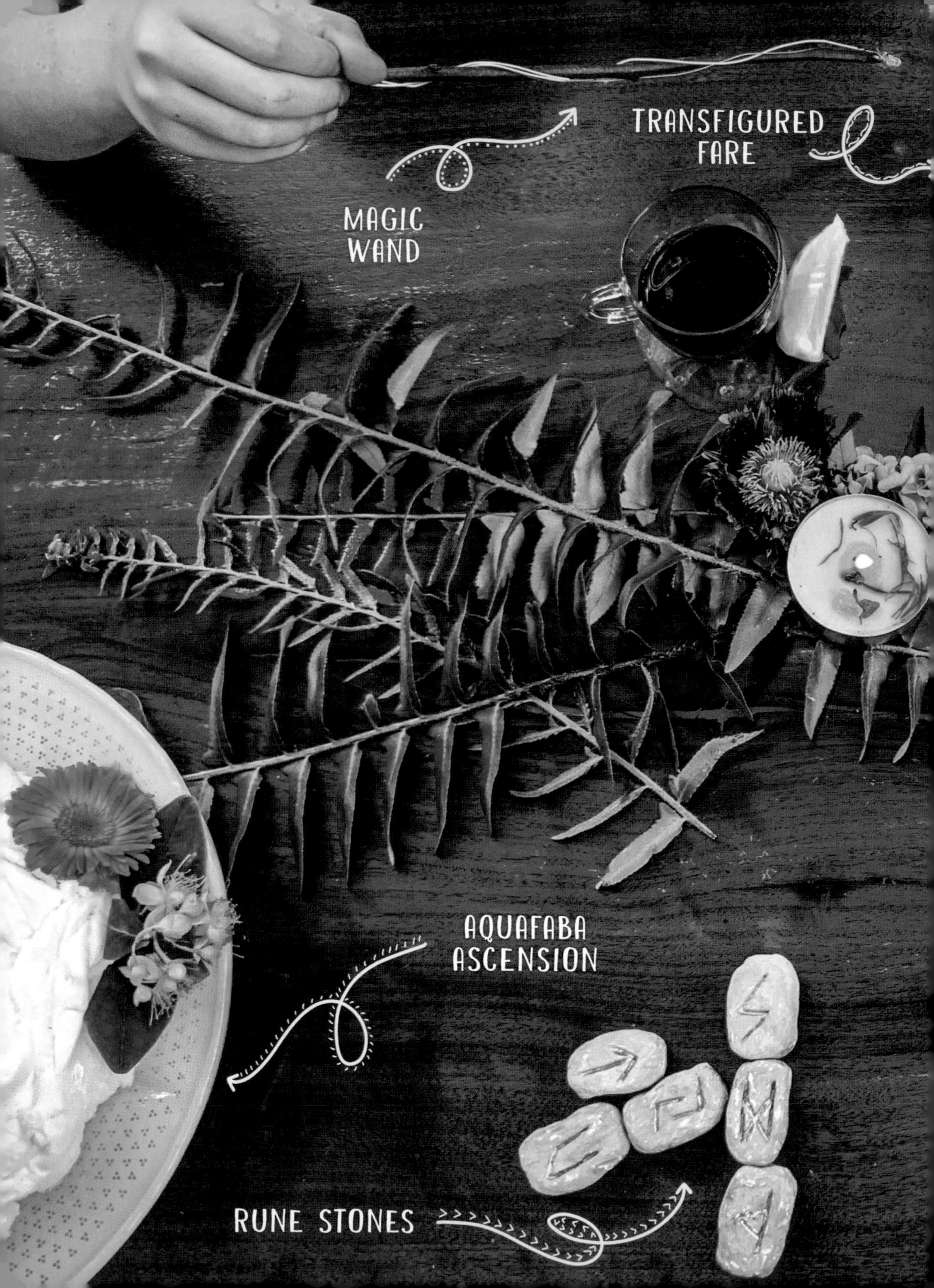

MAGIC
WAND

TRANSFIGURED
FARE

AQUAFABA
ASCENSION

RUNE STONES

ELIXIR OF
ENLIGHTENMENT

ASTRAL
INVOCATION

SORCERER'S
STONE

FORGE OF THE
MICROBES

FOREWORD FOR CAREGIVERS

Nature has long captivated our attention and imagination. Our draw to the Earth and our fascination with mysterious happenings in the natural world create an urge to explore their pairing. This has manifested itself as magic throughout history. From witches to alchemists to healers, magic has been a way to explain the phenomena that can be conjured from our natural world. As science and technology have crept into our societies, many enchantments have been unveiled by theories and experiments. We began to understand the interaction of molecules and matter, and the mystery of magic gave way to the underlying science. However, the draw to the unknown is undeniable to some of us. This book seeks to showcase the science behind seemingly magical activities while still embracing the excitement and connection with nature that magic affords. It hopes to show that science is not incompatible with our innate draw to nature but an extension of it. Giving children the opportunity to explore this connection will allow them to see the science all around them. Childhood is a time of preparation for adulthood but more so a time to embrace and encourage the overwhelming urge to explore, create, learn, and imagine. Please enjoy this adventure into the molecular, atomic, and subatomic world as we pair technology and nature to bring you some truly enchanted science.

HOW TO USE THiS BOOK

Creativity and awe are integral traits of any successful scientist, and they are rooted in the imaginative exercises of childhood. This book is meant to stimulate the imagination while giving opportunities to apply it creatively and concretely. It also serves to give a tour of the science of our world, dabbling in concepts from chaos theory to basic chemical reactions. It illustrates that learning the scientific reasoning behind a mysterious event does not take away from the magic but instead exposes more exciting mysteries and questions to be answered. Use these projects to encourage imaginative and dramatic play with the things you create, use the raw materials to experiment and create more curiosities, and allow the child to lead the way.

Each chapter highlights a natural phenomenon inspired by magic: Infusions (pH and indicators), Illumination (light), Sorcery (forces), Alchemy (physical and chemical changes), and Mimicry (biology-inspired engineering). The introductions of each section include interesting snippets about the historical aspects of the magic along with an overview of the scientific concepts. Additional, more-specific information is given on each activity page.

Rhyming, rhythmic incantations are one of the most well-known parts of magical play, and each activity includes a spell to chant. These are not quite traditional spells, however, and are actually scientific explanations of the project. See if you can glean the meaning of each line after you perform the activity.

WHAT TO KEEP IN YOUR CUPBOARD

Butterfly pea tea

Butterfly pea is the common name for the plant *Clitoria ternatea*, which is native to Southeast Asia. It can be purchased from online retailers or specialty grocery stores.

DRIED BUTTERFLY PEA FLOWER TEA

Ground turmeric

Turmeric is a brightly colored spice made from the root of the plant *Curcuma longa*. It can be found in your local supermarket spice aisle.

TURMERIC

Citric acid

Citric acid is a naturally occurring organic acid used in foods and beverages, cosmetics, and pharmaceuticals. It is found in citrus fruits like lemons, limes, and oranges and is also an important molecule in human metabolism. Most citric acid used today is produced by a fungus, then purified. Citric acid can be purchased at supermarkets in the spice or canning aisles. It is also available from online retailers.

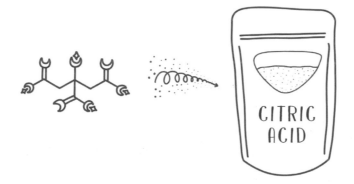

Washing soda

Washing soda is an inorganic compound commonly used in laundry detergents. It can be purchased in the detergent aisle. You can also make washing soda by baking a thin layer of baking soda at 400°F for 30 minutes.

Cream of tartar

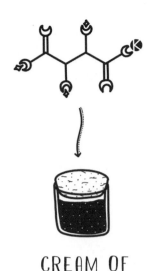

CREAM OF TARTAR

Cream of tartar is an organic acid found on the inside of wine casks. It has become a common ingredient in many recipes. It can be found in the spice and baking aisle of your supermarket.

Rubbing alcohol

Rubbing alcohol, also known as isopropanol or isopropyl alcohol, is a commonly used antiseptic for cuts and scrapes. It can be purchased in the first aid aisle of a supermarket or pharmacy.

RUBBING ALCOHOL

(ISOPROPANOL)

Glycerol

Glycerol, also known as glycerin, is a common additive in cosmetics and medicines. It is a compound left over from the traditional soap-making process. It can be purchased from pharmacies, many supermarkets, or online retailers.

GLYCEROL

LEDs

LEDs, short for light emitting diodes, are a type of light source. They can be found in a range of colors and sizes. For these projects, you will want small 5 mm LEDs. They can be purchased from online retailers or hobby stores.

Alligator clips

Alligator clips are clip-on wires that are used to easily create temporary electrical circuits. They can be purchased from big-box stores or online retailers.

Hobby motors

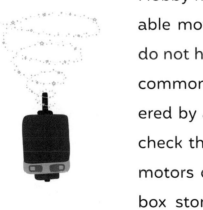

Hobby motors are small, easily operable motors that spin fairly fast but do not have a lot of power. The most common hobby motors can be powered by a 9 V battery, but be sure to check the operator's manual. Hobby motors can be purchased from big-box stores, hobby stores, or online retailers.

Switches

Switches are devices used to turn a circuit on and off. They physically open and close a wire in the circuit so electrons cannot pass through. Switches can be purchased from hobby stores or online retailers, but they can easily be made for these projects from conductive household items like paper clips.

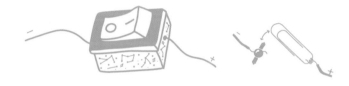

INFUSiONS

A glimpse out the window reveals the incredible diversity of life here on Earth. Nature has given us countless tastes, smells, colors, shapes, and textures. If we look closer, we can see that this diversity arises from molecular diversity—life is so varied because it can create so many different molecules. Each organism in nature is like a tiny factory, churning out molecules it may need to survive, some of which we can extract and harness through infusions. In this chapter, you will use amazing molecules extracted from natural products to perform feats of magical chemistry.

PLANTS AS MEDICINE

Observers throughout history have noticed peculiar results from consuming certain plants—some could cause harm, and some could heal. After much trial and error, healers and apothecaries developed assortments of plants to use for everything from stomachaches to love potions. These medicinal traits have created a mystical aura around nature, but we now know that these phenomena are simply caused by molecules in the plants interacting with the molecules in our bodies. Though many herbal remedies of the past have proved ineffective, there are many examples that showed promise. Modern science has used these effective historical remedies as inspiration for pharmaceuticals. The active molecule in aspirin was found in willow bark, which was chewed by ancient people for millennia. Digitalis is a beautifully

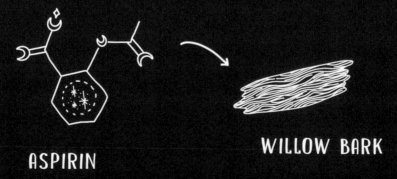

ASPIRIN   WILLOW BARK

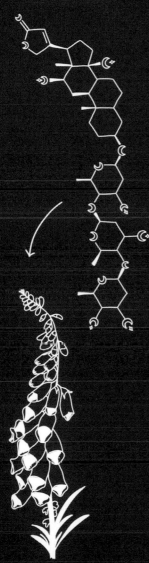

DIGITALIS

FOXGLOVE

flowering yet toxic plant, often called foxglove. A molecule from digitalis causes a stronger heartbeat and was used by ancient healers, but it was dangerous, as even a small amount can be deadly. Fortunately, when carefully prepared with modern scientific techniques, digitalis is now a drug used to treat heart failure.

Beyond pharmaceuticals, other examples of fascinating molecules created by plants are pigments—brightly colored compounds often used by the plant world to attract pollinators like the honeybee. Humans have used them to dye fabric, formulate makeup, and create art. Some of these compounds have an additional feature—they can change color when exposed to an acid or base. These are called indicators. You will utilize this property to perform spells with indicative infusions!

ACiDS AND BASES

Before we explore indicators, we must first learn about acids and bases, the compounds that cause indicators to change color. You have encountered some of these compounds before. Lemon juice and vinegar are acids, while baking soda and many detergents are bases.

Acids and bases are molecules or minerals. There are little parts of molecules called protons. Protons are very tiny, but their presence or absence can make a huge difference in how that molecule behaves. In one theory, acids can give a proton to a molecule, and bases can accept a proton.

These little changes can have big effects! While acids and bases can cause damage by shuffling around protons that shouldn't have been shuffled, we can also use acids and bases to our benefit. We can use acid to add flavor to a meal or bases to make soap from fats. Chemists use acids and bases all the time in their laboratories, and you will use them here to modify your indicative infusions!

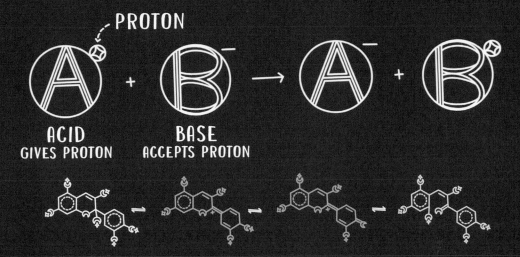

PROTON

ACID
GIVES PROTON

BASE
ACCEPTS PROTON

The molecules that change color when exposed to acids or bases create a vivid and confusing effect if one is not aware of the science behind the phenomenon. These special molecules are called indicators because they indicate that an acid or base is present. They can also tell us about a value called pH, which is a measure of how many protons are present in the solution. The lower the pH, the more protons are present in the solution. Different indicators change color at different pH values.

You can make your own indicators at home by using one of several common plant parts, like red cabbage or the spice turmeric. There are many tricks you can perform using these color transformations too! In this chapter, you will explore five projects that use natural indicators to enchant and amaze.

Low pH —————— High pH

RED CABBAGE

ONION SKINS

Low pH —————— High pH

Low pH

FOUND IN NATURE

BUTTERFLY PEA FLOWER

High pH

Low pH ——————— High pH

BLUEBERRY

Low pH ——————— High pH

TURMERIC

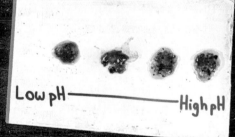

ELIXIR OF ENLIGHTENMENT

Infusion of ternatea, boil and steep,
partake with a friend you intend to keep.
Serve to them a tisane so blue,
add yellow acid, behold a pink brew.

BREW A STUNNING BLUE TEA THAT CHANGES COLOR WHEN AN EDIBLE ACID IS ADDED TO IT!

✧ Butterfly pea tea is made from the flowers of the plant *Clitoria ternatea*. It is native to Southeast Asia.

✧ Tisane: an infusion of plant parts in water.

✧ Ask an adult to help boil water.

CLITORIA
TERNATEA

SUPPLIES

- ✦ 2 cups water
- ✦ 2 teaspoons loose butterfly pea flowers (or 2 tea bags)
- ✦ Sugar or sweetener of choice (optional)
- ✦ Teacups (white or clear so the tea color is easy to see)
- ✦ Juice of 1 lemon

STEPS

1. Bring the water to a boil. Add the butterfly pea flowers. Let steep for 5 to 10 minutes, then remove the flowers. Add the sweetener if desired.
2. Pour into the cups, and note the blue color.
3. Add a small amount of lemon juice, and see it turn purple. Add even more lemon juice, and the tea will turn bright pink! Enjoy your potions with a friend.

SCIENCE

Butterfly pea tea is bright blue because of the presence of anthocyanins, which also happen to be pH indicators. Similar molecules are found in other foods like blueberries and cherries, though those forms appear as different colors. Lemon juice is an acid, which will lower the pH of the tisane. These acids can give protons to the anthocyanins and will change their color from blue to pink!

MASKED MESSAGE

Golden root, I create with thee
a tonic to reveal my decree.
My masked message is hidden from view.
Spill this potion, allow it to break through.

USE PH INDICATORS TO RELAY SECRET MESSAGES!

✧ Adult supervision required. Rubbing alcohol is flammable and should be used in a well-ventilated area. It is not be used around an open flame.

✧ Turmeric stains; be sure to protect your work surface and use recycled containers that you don't mind staining.

SUPPLIES

- 1 teaspoon ground turmeric
- 2 tablespoons rubbing alcohol
- Paintbrush
- Paper
- Yellow crayon
- 1 tablespoon baking soda
- ½ cup warm water
- Tray

TURMERIC

RUBBING
ALCOHOL

STEPS

1. Combine the turmeric and the rubbing alcohol in a recycled container, and swirl to mix. Let the turmeric solids settle.
2. Pour the (now yellow) rubbing alcohol into another container, being careful not to disturb the turmeric at the bottom of the cup.
3. Protect your work surface, and paint several sheets of paper completely yellow with the prepared solution. Allow to dry.

4. Use the crayon to write a message on the paper. It will be difficult to see what you wrote with the yellow crayon on the yellow paper.

5. Mix the baking soda into the warm water in another container.

6. Place the paper in the tray, and pour the baking soda solution over the paper to dramatically reveal your message. Alternatively, paint the baking soda solution over the paper, and watch the message appear.

SCIENCE

Turmeric contains the molecule curcumin, which is a pH indicator. It is yellow at acidic and neutral pH values and red at basic pH values. Curcumin is soluble in rubbing alcohol, so you can extract it from the turmeric and transfer it to the paper. The rubbing alcohol will evaporate, and you are left with curcumin-coated paper.

When you add the revealing solution, the baking soda accepts a proton from the curcumin molecule in the paper, turning the curcumin from yellow to red. Crayons are made of waxy substances that do not mix with water.

The wax blocks the baking soda solution from contacting the curcumin underneath and prevents the color change. Eventually, the solution absorbs through the paper under the crayon, making your message disappear slightly.

SPECTRAL BREATH

My breath transforms the liquid jewel.
Through air and lungs, the spell is fueled.
It bubbles through, the charms diffuse
to soft pink from vibrant blues.

USE YOUR BREATH TO CHANGE THE COLOR OF A SOLUTION!

SUPPLIES

- Red cabbage indicator solution
- Clear glass
- Water
- Baking soda
- Straw

MAKING RED CABBAGE INDICATOR SOLUTION

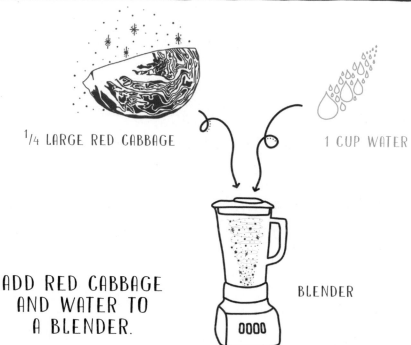

¹/₄ LARGE RED CABBAGE

1 CUP WATER

BLENDER

ADD RED CABBAGE AND WATER TO A BLENDER.

PULSE TILL CHOPPED.

POUR MIXTURE THROUGH A PAPER TOWEL AND STRAINER.

COLLECT THE LIQUID.

STEPS

1. Add a drop or so of indicator solution to a clear glass halfway full of water, enough that you can clearly see the color but not so much that it is dark. If your work surface is dark, place a white piece of paper underneath the glass. If the color is not already blue, mix a very small sprinkle of baking soda in until it just turns blue.
2. Add a straw, and blow into the solution. Keep blowing until the solution changes from blue to pink!

SCiENCE

When you exhale, your breath contains the gas carbon dioxide, CO_2. When carbon dioxide dissolves in water, it can react with the water to create an acid called carbonic acid. This acid then reacts with the anthocyanins from the red cabbage to turn them pink! The more indicator you add to the water, the more carbon dioxide you will have to blow into the liquid. Likewise, the more basic your tap water (or the more baking soda you add), the more you will have to blow. Experiment with different amounts of indicator or starting colors and note what happens!

This activity may be beautiful, but it also illustrates an unfortunate situation in our Earth's waters. Due to human activities, our atmosphere is accumulating increasing amounts of carbon dioxide that can dissolve in the oceans, causing them to acidify, just like this demonstration. This can damage marine life beyond repair.

COLOR INVERSION SPELL

A chameleon of a liquid dances through crystal lines.
An image appears as the magic combines.
Absorb, spread, react—the liquid snakes through.
What once was purple appears pink, green, and blue.

CREATE COLORFUL SALT-PAINTING ART USING ONLY ONE PAINT!

SUPPLIES

- ✦ 37 teaspoons table salt, divided
- ✦ 1 teaspoon citric acid
- ✦ 1 teaspoon baking soda
- ✦ 1 teaspoon washing soda
- ✦ Pencil
- ✦ Paper
- ✦ School glue
- ✦ Eyedropper or pipette
- ✦ Red cabbage indicator solution (see page 30 for recipe. You can also use butterfly pea tea.)

RED CABBAGE
INDICATOR SOLUTION

STEPS

1. Label four jars purple, pink, blue, and green.

2. To the purple jar, add 10 teaspoons table salt.

3. To the pink jar, add 9 teaspoons table salt and the citric acid.

4. To the blue jar, add 9 teaspoons table salt and the baking soda.

5. To the green jar, add 9 teaspoons table salt and the washing soda.

6. Plan a line drawing that has pink, purple, blue, and green as the colors. Lightly outline your drawing with a pencil on the paper.

7. Trace the line drawing with glue.

8. Sprinkle the salt mixtures carefully over the glue where each color is desired. For example, sprinkle the pink salt mix over each area that you want pink. Continue for each color. Work quickly but carefully.

9. Shake off the excess salt into the garbage, and allow the glue to dry.

10. Use the eyedropper or pipette to drop indicator solution onto the dried salt lines. Watch as the solution creeps through the salt and changes color!

SCiENCE

Red cabbage has a type of anthocyanin that can appear as several different colors based on the pH. Each of the salt mixes that you make will create a solution that has a different pH when dissolved in water. As you drop indicator solution onto the salt lines, some of the salts will dissolve in the water, changing the pH and reacting with the anthocyanin. The color of the indicator solution will reflect the pH of the solution, giving the effect of a magic color-changing drawing!

The solution appears to creep through the salt lines due to a process called absorption. Water in the indicator solution is attracted to the salt in the glue. This attraction is enough to guide the solution along the salt lines rather than pooling on the paper.

SANGUiNE ENERGY

Pungent fluid and longa root
capture the compound for it to transmute.
Energy flows, around the page it spreads.
That which was yellow now becomes red.

DRAW WITH ELECTRICITY!

✧ Adult supervision required. Rubbing alcohol is flammable and should be used in a well-ventilated area.
It is not be used around an open flame.

✧ Turmeric stains. Be sure to protect your workspace, and
use recycled containers that you don't mind staining.

✧ The spice turmeric is the root of
the plant *Curcuma longa*.

SUPPLiES

- ✦ 1 teaspoon ground turmeric
- ✦ 2 tablespoons rubbing alcohol
- ✦ Paintbrush
- ✦ Paper
- ✦ Baking sheet or aluminum foil larger than a sheet of paper
- ✦ 2 teaspoons salt
- ✦ ½ cup warm water
- ✦ Alligator clips
- ✦ 9 V battery

STEPS

1. Add the turmeric to the rubbing alcohol in a recycled container, and swirl to mix. Let the turmeric settle.

2. Pour the (now yellow) rubbing alcohol into another container, being careful not to disturb the turmeric at the bottom.

3. Protect your work surface, and paint several sheets

of paper completely yellow with the prepared solution. Allow to dry.

4. Put a sheet of yellow paper onto the baking sheet or foil.

5. Mix the salt into the warm water in another container.

6. Connect the alligator clips to the battery, then connect the alligator clip that is connected to the positive battery terminal to the baking sheet or foil.

7. Add a spoonful of the salt water to the yellow paper, and spread to dampen.

8. Touch the negative alligator clip to the yellow paper. A red mark should appear. Now draw a picture or write a message!

✧ For a trick, you can clip an unfolded paper clip to the negative alligator clip, then tape the alligator clip to your palm and the paper clip to your index finger, then make it look like you are writing with your finger!

SCiENCE

When you touch the negative alligator clip to the paper, you are completing the circuit. This allows electrons to flow from the negative terminal on the battery, through the wire, through the yellow paper and salt solution, through the baking sheet and wire, and into the positive terminal of the battery. Along the way, some of the electrons react with the water and produce hydroxyl ions, which are bases. These react with the indicator, curcumin, and turn it red!

TRANSFiGURED FARE

We take food from the Earth to nurture and nourish,
we take dye from the Earth that has grown and flourished.
Blend them together and we will discover
the colors that emerge once uncovered.

ENJOY A COLOR-CHANGING SNACK!

✧ The darker the dye of the food, the more acid or base you will need to see the color change. Deep colors are beautiful, but it may take a minute to see the color change when compared to less saturated batches.

SUPPLIES

- ✦ Butterfly pea flowers or red cabbage juice for indicator solution
- ✦ Pasta, white rice, rice noodles, or rice paper wrappers
- ✦ An edible acid, like lemon juice or a light-colored vinegar
- ✦ Baking soda
- ✦ Water

STEPS

1. If using butterfly pea flowers, add 1 to 2 tablespoons of butterfly pea flowers per cup of boiling water and let steep for 15 minutes. If using red cabbage, prepare the indicator solution used in the Spectral Breath activity according to page 28. Make enough indicator solution to replace the water when preparing the food of choice. (For example, boil 1 cup of rice in 2 cups of indicator solution instead of 2 cups of water, or soak rice noodles in 2 cups hot indicator solution instead of hot water.)

2. Prepare the rice or pasta dish of choice with the indicator solution.
3. Add 1 tsp baking soda to ½ cup warm water and stir till dissolved. Use as your base.
4. Cut and squeeze the lemon into a bowl, or add vinegar to a bowl for your acid.
5. Serve the colored food in a wide bowl or dish. Add drops and splashes of the edible acids and base and observe how they change the color of your food.
6. When ready to eat, enjoy the dish as is or add additional flavorings like spices or oils.

SCIENCE

Indicators, or compounds that change color in response to an acid or base, are very useful in a laboratory setting. Scientists often need to check the pH of a solution, and indicators are an inexpensive and easy option. Serendipitously, several indicators, acids, and bases are found in edible products that allow us to experiment and have fun with color-changing food. Note how the acids and bases feel on your fingers and taste in your mouth. Before the advent of modern analytical tools, many scientists would feel and taste compounds to discern if they were an acid or a base! Scientists no longer do this as many chemical compounds are toxic to humans.

ILLUMiNATiON

Controlling light is a powerful form of magic. Light gives us life, safety, and warmth. Though we see it every day, it can easily be transformed from the mundane to the magical.

CELESTIAL LIGHT

The Sun and Moon are seemingly suspended in our sky, but we of course know that the Earth rotates around the Sun, and the Moon rotates around the Earth. But what if no one ever told you this? If you sit outside and look at the movements of our celestial bodies, it really seems as if the Sun and Moon are rotating around Earth. Several keen minds throughout human history had found after closer study that the Earth does in fact revolve around the sun, but it wasn't until a few hundred years ago that this was widely accepted. Long ago, most people had supernatural understandings of the heavens, which made events dealing with the sky very striking to them. Imagine their reaction when an eclipse occurred!

Lunar eclipses occur when the Earth blocks the Sun from shining on the Moon. A solar eclipse is when the Moon blocks the Sun from shining on a small part of the Earth. These are now predictable events because we can solve equations to estimate each body's position in space, but in the past, most people did not have knowledge of astronomy. Solar eclipses are thought to have been terrifying events, rare enough that people

LUNAR
ECLIPSE

SOLAR
ECLIPSE

may only see one in a lifetime, with no warning before it occurred. Many did not know whether the sun or moon would return. Myths and rituals were built around these events, because there was limited knowledge of what was actually happening.

In modern days, eclipses are an exciting event. We are confident the Sun and Moon will be revealed again, and we are taught to view the celestial bodies safely. The history of eclipses, though, is a prime example of the power of knowledge.

Though the sun is our most prominent light source, there are many other ways to create light and many other ways to create magical happenings with it too. In this chapter, you will discover several ways to create, use, and control light. Light has enchanted humans throughout history, and as we delve into a deeper understanding of the phenomenon, we are only met with more amazement.

LiGHT

Light is made of mysterious things called photons. There are many ways to create photons, which can be considered tiny packets of energy. Nuclear reactions in the sun create the photons in sunlight that we see and feel on Earth, and chemical reactions create the photons that cause fireflies to light up the forest, to name a few.

Some photons have more energy than others. Low-energy photons include microwaves and radio waves, while high-energy photons include X-rays and gamma

rays. All these energetic photons are part of the electromagnetic spectrum. The light we see is actually only from a very narrow portion of the spectrum. Try to imagine your surroundings as if you had the ability to see more wavelengths of light. There are microwaves left over from the Big Bang that still hit the Earth; what would it look like to see them? Flowers have designs in ultraviolet (UV),

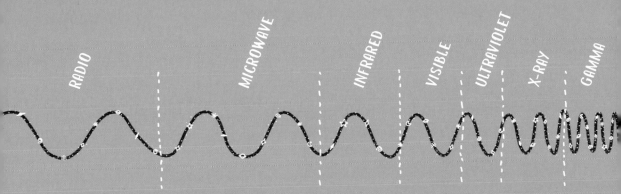

RADIO MICROWAVE INFRARED VISIBLE ULTRAVIOLET X-RAY GAMMA

a type of light that humans cannot see but can be seen by pollinators. How different would our world look if we could see those photons?

Photons are carriers of energy, so making photons needs energy. In these projects, you will be using power sources such as batteries, the sun, and chemical bonds to experiment with light. By understanding the science behind a light source, you can manipulate materials to create some magic of your own!

SPELLBOUND CIRCUIT

Draw the path for the energy carrier,
a continuous line with no barrier.
Apply the source of charge and flow.
Make this creation come alive and glow.

+   −

+ ─▷|─ −

DRAW THE CONDUCTORS OF A
CIRCUIT USING A PENCIL!

✧ LED stands for light emitting diode. Electrons that pass through the LED cause the semiconductor material inside to emit light. Current can pass through only in one direction, though, so the negative side of the LED needs to connect to the negative side of the battery, or else it won't turn on.

✧ Basic circuits contain a power source, conductive material, and an electrical load. The power source provides the electricity to power the circuit. The conductive material carries the electricity around the circuit. The electrical load, like an LED or motor, uses the electricity to perform a function. You will be assembling several circuits throughout this book.

CIRCUITS

BATTERY

LED

WIRE

✧ Usually in electronics projects, you cannot use a 9 V battery with one ~3 V LED with no added components, but the graphite in this project resists the flow of electrons enough that a 9 V is necessary to turn on the LED.

SUPPLIES

- Pencil
- Paper
- 5 mm LED, approx. 3 V
- Clear Scotch tape
- 9 V battery

STEPS

1. Make a line drawing that forms a continuous shape, but leave two small gaps about ¼ inch wide. One gap will be bridged by the battery and the other by the LED.

2. Make the line about ¼ inch thick, and color it in darkly using the pencil so no paper shows beneath the line.

3. Splay the legs of the LED, and bend them into a right angle. Note that the positive leg is the longer leg, and the negative leg is the shorter leg. Tape the LED so it spans the gap on the drawing, making sure the legs are in good contact with the lines. Mark the positive and negative legs.

4. Place the battery on the other gap, with the negative terminal touching the line that leads to the negative leg and the positive terminal on the positive line. The LED should light up!

SCiENCE

The graphite from pencils is a poor conductor of electricity but a conductor nonetheless! The graphite lines that you draw allow electrons to flow from the battery into the LED, letting you make some pretty inventive circuits. To experiment with this system, try making a small circular circuit and a large circular circuit (remembering to add the two gaps) and comparing the brightness of the LED. Also try varying the thickness of the line and how dark you make it. What do your results suggest? To take it a step further, can you make 3D circuits using this technique?

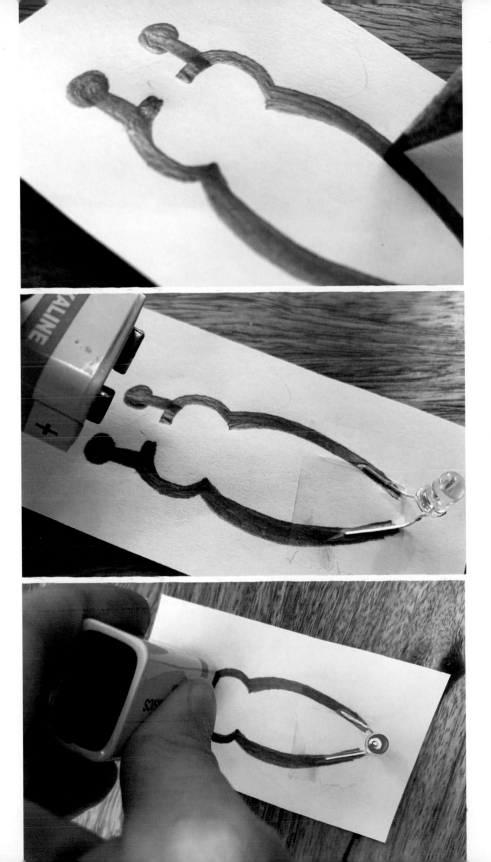

MAGIC WAND

Grasp the wand; there's only one it knows.
The right enchanter makes energy flow.
Metal touches metal; the circle is complete.
That which is stored will begin to deplete.

CREATE A MAGIC WAND THAT WILL LIGHT UP WHEN YOU GRASP THE STICK IN A CERTAIN WAY!

✧ Button cell batteries are very dangerous when swallowed. In addition to being a choking hazard, they can cause severe internal burns. Do not use around small children, and do not leave the batteries unattended. Two AAA batteries in a holder with leads can be used in their place.

✧ This activity was inspired by several types of bioluminescent bacteria and fungi that can give earthly objects like wood a supernatural glow.

SUPPLIES

- ✦ 5 mm LED, approx. 3 V, in color of choice
- ✦ Stick
- ✦ Copper tape or insulated wire
- ✦ Tape
- ✦ 3 V button cell battery
- ✦ Various decorations

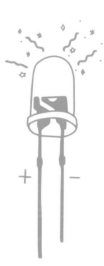

STEPS

1. Plan where each part of the circuit will go on your stick. You want the battery to lie right where your hand will hold the stick so the pressure of your grasp will touch a wire to the battery and complete the circuit.

2. Splay the legs of the LED slightly, and tape it to the tip of the stick.

3. Measure two lengths of copper tape or wire so they stretch from the LED legs down to where you want to put your battery. Attach the wires to each leg of the LED with tape.

4. Affix the end of the wire that leads to the negative LED leg to where you would like the battery to be placed. Tightly secure the battery over an exposed part of that negative wire, ensuring the negative side of the battery is touching it.

5. Position the positive wire so that it hangs just above the positive side of the battery. When pressed onto the battery, it should light up the LED. If desired, affix a decoration to disguise the battery.

6. Decorate the rest of your wand, and try it out!

SCiENCE

When you grasp your wand in the correct way to press the wire against the battery, you are completing the circuit to allow electrons to pass from the battery, through the LED, then back to the battery, making it appear as though you have a magical touch to activate your wand! What else can you make light up?

FLUORESCENT FEAST

Escape the visible realm that confines.
Though we cannot see, still it shines.
Illuminate the once mundane.
The feast we share, a glow it gains.

CREATE A MEAL THAT GLOWS UNDER A BLACK LIGHT!

✧ Ask an adult to help use the stove.

✧ UV light is an invisible type of electromagnetic radiation. It is the next highest in energy after visible light.

✧ A black light shines low-energy UV light. Though it is fine for your skin for the duration of a meal, don't look directly into the light.

VISIBLE   ULTRAVIOLET

✧ Though humans cannot see UV light, other animals can. For example, many pollinators, such as bees and butterflies, can see UV light. Flowers sometimes have UV-active marking on them, possibly to attract these pollinators.

✧ Fluorescence is when a molecule absorbs a photon, then sends back out a lower energy photon. Highlighters seem to be brighter than other markers because they can create light from the light shining on them. Take a look at highlighters under a black light to really see this effect!

FLUORESCENCE

SUPPLiES

- ✦ Pasta Sauce
  - ✧ 2 cups fresh basil leaves
  - ✧ 2 tablespoons pine nuts or walnuts
  - ✧ 2 cloves garlic
  - ✧ ¼ teaspoon salt
  - ✧ ¾ cup olive oil
- ✦ 3 tablespoons butter, room temperature
- ✦ 1 teaspoon turmeric
- ✦ Pasta of choice
- ✦ Tonic water
- ✦ Ice
- ✦ Lime wedges
- ✦ Olive oil
- ✦ Bread or rolls
- ✦ Black light

STEPS

1. Add the basil, nuts, garlic, and salt to a food processor and turn it on. While it's running, slowly add the olive oil. Set aside.
2. Mix the softened butter and turmeric together in a small bowl. Set aside.
3. Cook the pasta according to the directions and strain. Toss with the prepared olive oil sauce.
4. Pour the tonic water into glasses and add ice and lime wedges.
5. Serve the pasta with additional olive oil on top to increase the fluorescence. Serve the bread or rolls with the turmeric butter.
6. Hang the black light over the dining area in a dark room.
7. Turn on the black light and turn off the normal lights to see your glowing food!

SCiENCE

Plants make many organic molecules besides the familiar vitamins, carbohydrates, fats, and proteins. Some of these molecules are fluorescent, which means they can take light of a certain energy and emit it as lower energy light. In this activity, you are seeing fluorescence from the molecules of curcumin in the turmeric, chlorophyll from the basil and olive oil in the pesto, and quinine in the tonic water. These molecules take UV light and emit it as visible light. Since our eyes cannot see the UV light shining on the food but can see the visible light shining back from the food, it looks like light is magically emanating! Explore your pantry and art supplies, and see what other items fluoresce!

CHLOROPHYLL

CURCUMIN

QUININE

ASTRAL INVOCATION

Channel the power of the nearest star.
The vessel captures energy from afar.
Transfer the vibrations into the wax.
Create a beacon with which to relax.

MAKE YOUR OWN CANDLES WITH A SOLAR OVEN!

✧ Adult supervision required. The solar oven can reach high temperatures and may cause burns. Always ask permission to burn the candle you make.

✧ The sun's light and heat are created by hydrogen atoms coming together to form helium. This is called nuclear fusion, and it releases an immense amount of energy.

✧ Sunlight hits the Earth and can transfer its energy to the material it hits. Light can also reflect off certain surfaces to direct the energy.

✧ When molecules vibrate in a certain way, we feel this movement as heat.

SUPPLIES

+ Cardboard box
+ Aluminum foil
+ Strong tape, like duct tape
+ Black paint or paper
+ Candle container or jar
+ Wicks
+ Sticks/pencils/clothespins
+ Long sticks
+ Candle wax
+ Essential oil (optional)
+ Wax colorant (optional)
+ Decorations like dried flowers or glitter

STEPS

1. Cover the inner sides and the flaps of the box with aluminum foil, securing with tape where necessary. Paint the inside bottom of the box black or cover with black paper.
2. Prepare your candle jars by suspending the wick over the middle of the jar using a stick, pencil, or clothespin.
3. Position the box so the base gets direct sunlight. Using the long sticks, prop up the flaps so they reflect sun into the box.
4. Add the wax to a heat-safe container that will fit in the box and place into the solar oven. Let the wax melt, carefully stirring when needed.
5. Remove the melted wax from the solar oven, and add scents or colorant if desired.
6. Pour the wax into the jars, decorate the tops, and let dry. Trim the wicks.

SCIENCE

The sun gets its energy from nuclear fusion reactions, and some of this energy, in the form of electromagnetic radiation, reaches the Earth. We see most of this energy as visible light, but there are also other components such as UV light and infrared light. When light hits a material, some of the molecules can absorb the light as energy and vibrate. This vibration causes molecules to bump into one another, increasing the kinetic energy of the system, the space between the molecules, and the temperature of the material.

The foil flaps on the solar oven reflect the sun's energy into the box, adding more heat to the system than there would be without the flaps. In addition, the black bottom further helps absorb the heat, because black items absorb all visible light. It therefore gets quite hot inside the box. Your new candles will all be thanks to nuclear reactions in the sun!

You can expand this activity by cooking s'mores or melting cheese for pizzas in the solar oven. You can also experiment by comparing oven temperatures with and without flaps and with different colored paper at the bottom.

EXTINGUISHING EFFERVESCENCE

From nahcolite and secretion of a wee beast
evolve an ethereal gas that will be released.
Poured onto flame, it will douse and smother
but will not be seen by any other.

COMBINE BAKING SODA AND VINEGAR TO CREATE CARBON DIOXIDE, THEN USE IT TO EXTINGUISH A FLAME WITHOUT TOUCHING IT!

✧ Adult supervision required.

✧ Baking soda, $NaHCO_3$, also called sodium bicarbonate, is found in nature as the mineral nahcolite.

✧ Vinegar is made from acetic acid bacteria, which is a group of bacteria that can take alcohols and sugars and secrete acetic acid.

SUPPLIES

- 3 candles
- ½ cup vinegar
- 2 tablespoons baking soda
- Tall container with lid

STEPS

1. Ask an adult to help light the candles.
2. Add the vinegar to the tall container.
3. Slowly add the baking soda, and loosely cover the container with the lid (do not seal). Wait till fizzing has stopped, then add the rest of the baking soda.
4. Remove the lid, and without pouring out the liquid, slowly pour the vapor over the candles and watch them extinguish!

SCiENCE

The reaction of vinegar and baking soda creates water and carbon dioxide, which is an invisible gas. Carbon dioxide is heavier than air, so it will stay in the container for a bit unless it is disturbed. When you "pour" it out, the carbon dioxide sinks down on top of the candles, pushing oxygen away from the fire. Fire needs oxygen to burn, so the flames go out.

GLOWING GAUNTLETS

Power on one, light on the next.
Hand over hand, see the effects.
The conduit wraps 'round wrists of the strong
signaling courage and bravery that was there all along.

CREATE BRACELETS THAT LIGHT UP WHEN YOU CROSS YOUR WRISTS!

✧ Adult supervision required. Button cell batteries are very dangerous when swallowed. In addition to being a choking hazard, they can cause severe internal burns. Do not use around small children and do not leave the batteries unattended. Two AAA batteries in a holder with leads can be used in their place, if preferred.

SUPPLiES

- ✦ Thick paper or card stock
- ✦ Copper tape or insulated wire
- ✦ 3 V button cell battery
- ✦ 5 mm LED in color of choice
- ✦ Tape
- ✦ Markers and various decorations

STEPS

1. Measure your wrists and cut paper to fit according to diagram 1.
2. Decide if you would like your bracelets to light up with your wrists crossed outstretched in front of you (option A) or crossed in front of your chest (option B). Follow the respective diagrams for each option.
3. Splay the legs of the LED and tape them on top of the copper tape on the correct piece of paper, noting the polarity, as in diagram 2.
4. Peel and stick copper tape according to diagram 3,

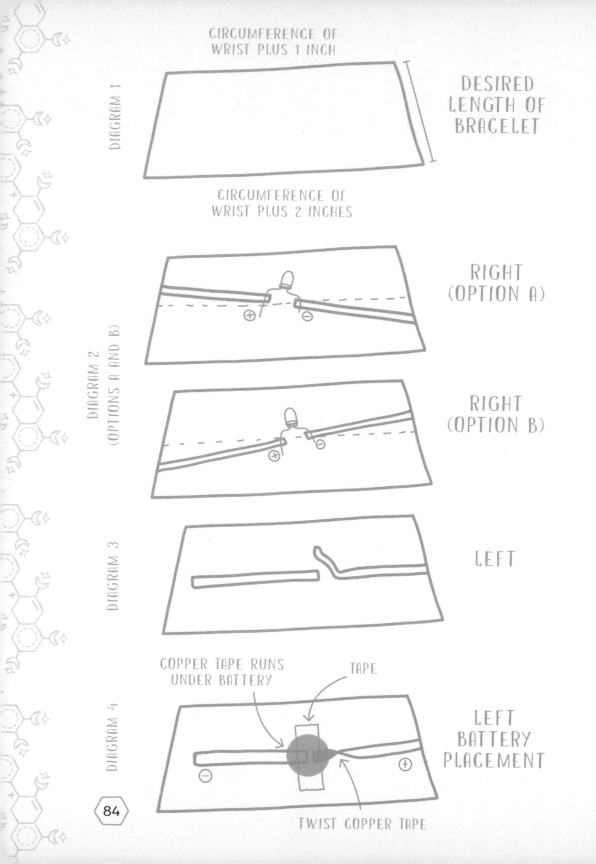

CIRCUMFERENCE OF
WRIST PLUS 1 INCH

DIAGRAM 1

DESIRED
LENGTH OF
BRACELET

CIRCUMFERENCE OF
WRIST PLUS 2 INCHES

DIAGRAM 2
(OPTIONS A AND B)

RIGHT
(OPTION A)

RIGHT
(OPTION B)

DIAGRAM 3

LEFT

COPPER TAPE RUNS
UNDER BATTERY

TAPE

DIAGRAM 4

LEFT
BATTERY
PLACEMENT

TWIST COPPER TAPE

leaving an unstuck "tail" of one side of the copper tape on the left bracelet to affix to the battery.

5. Position the battery positive side up, as shown in diagram 4. Be sure the negative bottom side of the battery is in contact with the copper tape. Flip the unstuck copper tape tail over so the more conductive side is in contact with the positive side of the battery. Tape it in place, then tape the battery in place.

6. Decorate your bracelets if desired.

7. Wrap the bracelets around your wrists and tape them closed. Put the LED bracelet on the right hand with the LED on the top side of the wrist. Put the battery bracelet on the left hand with the battery on the bottom side of the wrist.

8. Lay your right wrist over your left in the position you chose and illuminate your bracelet!

SCIENCE

In this circuit, your arms are acting as the switch. When they are apart, the circuit is incomplete and off. When you place them together the correct way, you complete the circuit and the LED turns on! What other wearable circuits can you dream up using this strategy?

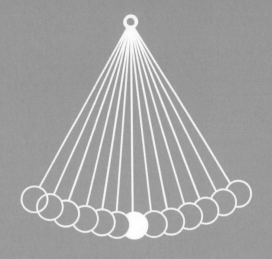

SORCERY

Often in magical scenes, we see a force being exerted on something without touching it—a fireball being propelled though the air or someone levitating an object. A force is an interaction between objects that causes a push or a pull. We usually experience forces when something physically touches us, but there are examples of forces in real life that can act at a distance without making any contact, such as gravity or magnetism. Forces can be manipulated in ways to make a system appear quite magical. Just a simple demonstration of an unfamiliar force could seem like a spell has been cast.

LODESTONES

Long ago, people were unfamiliar with invisible forces such as magnetism. The first magnets were found as rare, naturally magnetic stones called lodestones. Although they look like normal stones, they could attract iron-containing materials and were able to orient with the Earth's magnetic field. Soon, people realized they could magnetize other iron-containing items using a lodestone and create compasses to help navigate. Having the ability to exert a force without touch, magnets were thought to be magical and were used from everything from healing to trickery. Devices employing lodestones could be used in the practice of divination, the presumed use of the supernatural to seek guidance. Imagine a lodestone being used to turn an iron-containing item—it would seem as if a super-natural power was trying to communicate if you didn't know about magnetism! Eventually, humans learned that magnetism could be created in many ways, and we now have a range of magnets available to us. In this chapter, you will be using forces like magnetism to create your own spellbinding effects.

UNSEEN FORCES

All matter interacts through four fundamental forces: gravity, electromagnetism, the weak nuclear force, and the strong nuclear force. Everything we can observe can be described using a combination of these four forces, from the movement of the planets to your finger feeling the texture of this page.

✦ Gravity: A force that causes objects with mass or energy to be attracted to each other.

GRAVITY

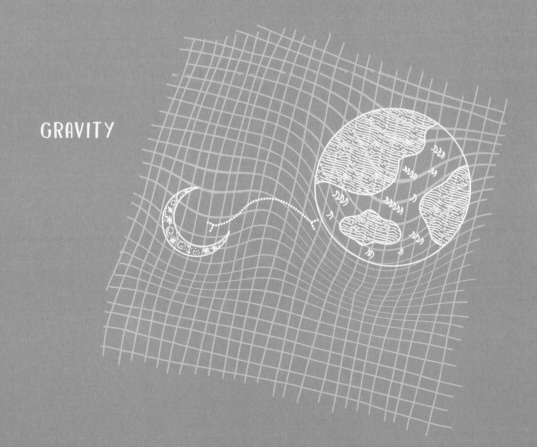

✦ Electromagnetism: A force that causes charged particles to attract or repel each other.

ELECTROMAGNETISM

✦ Strong nuclear force: A force that keeps protons and neutrons together in the nucleus of atoms.

STRONG NUCLEAR FORCE

✦ Weak nuclear force: A force that governs subatomic particles.

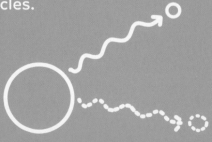

WEAK NUCLEAR FORCE

Magnetism is a result of the electromagnetic force. Objects contain electrons, which are negatively charged particles. Negatively charged particles repel other negatively charged particles according to the electromagnetic force. In magnetic objects, the electrons are arranged in such a way that they can apply the attractive or repulsive force of electromagnetism all together at a distance, whereas nonmagnetic objects have electrons that are arranged more randomly and do not exert a force together. The area in which the electromagnetic force of a magnet can be felt by other charged particles is called the magnetic field.

MAGNETISM

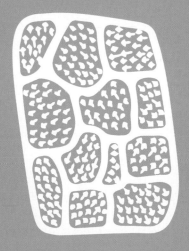

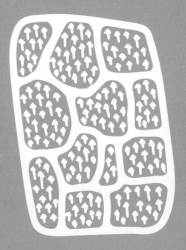

UNMAGNETIZED   MAGNETIZED

Electricity is a result of the electromagnetic force. Electrons are negatively charged and can flow through a conductive material toward a positively charged point, which is often the positive terminal of a battery.

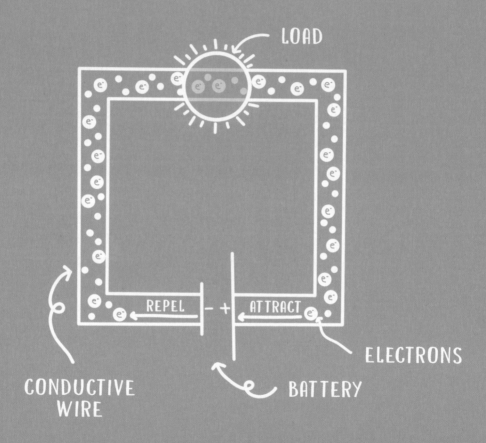

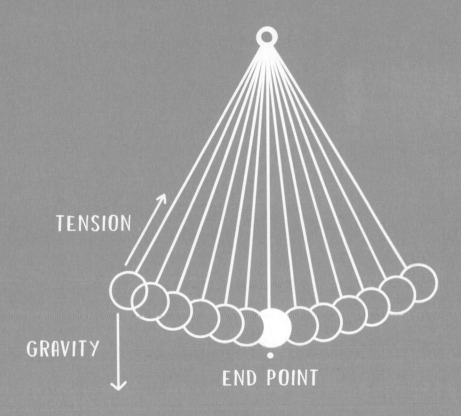

TENSION

GRAVITY

END POINT

A pendulum swinging is a result of gravity and the electromagnetic force. The gravity of the Earth pulls the pendulum mass, eventually settling at the point closest to the Earth. The swinging is made possible by chemical bonds in the string that are the result of the electromagnetic force.

From the vibration of an off-balance motor to the designs of paint on a spinning paper, can you divine the forces at work in the following projects?

GRAVITATIONAL FORCE

The force of attraction between everything with mass.

If you dropped these items off a building, they would catch the air differently and fall at different rates. This is called air resistance. If you could drop them all in a room with no air, called a vacuum, they would all fall at the same rate! This is due to an interplay between the difficulty of moving an object of greater mass and the fact that gravity pulls harder on the more massive object. It all balances, and all the items would fall at the same rate!

Electromagnetism is responsible for the attraction between molecules. It is the force behind why things like pine sap are sticky!

THE STRONG FORCE

The force that holds together protons and neutrons in the nucleus of an atom. It is also responsible for holding together the things that make up protons and neutrons, called quarks!

ELECTROMAGNETIC FORCE

A force between charged particles. Opposite charges attract and the same type of charges repel.

Photons, which create the light and colors all around us, are the force carrier for the electromagnetic force.

Magnetism is also brought about by this force.

THE WEAK FORCE

A mysterious force that has been full of surprises for physicists. A result of this force is a radioactive decay called beta-decay where a subatomic particle can turn into a different type of particle. Scientist measure this change to estimate the age of bones.

This force is also responsible for chemical reactions, like combustion!

THE ORACLE

Eccentric rotation creates a chaotic wanderer.
Intent is clear, though, with a skilled conjurer.
Ask the oracle for yeses and noes.
She holds the answer to the questions you pose.

TURN A CLASSIC WIGGLE-BOT INTO A FUTURE-PREDICTING GAME!

✧ Adult supervision required. Ask an adult to help cut the cork.

SUPPLIES

- ✦ Markers or paint
- ✦ Shallow cardboard box
- ✦ Hobby motor
- ✦ Hot glue
- ✦ 9 V battery
- ✦ 9 V battery clip with lead wires
- ✦ Switch
- ✦ Something to make the body and legs of the wiggle-bot (piece of wood and corks, recycled plastic cup and bottle caps, etc.)
- ✦ Cork
- ✦ Razor blade or knife
- ✦ Pen

STEPS

1. Draw or paint "Yes" and "No" on the inside bottom of the cardboard box. Feel free to add more options like "Maybe" and decorate the box!
2. Assemble the motor circuit according to the diagram.

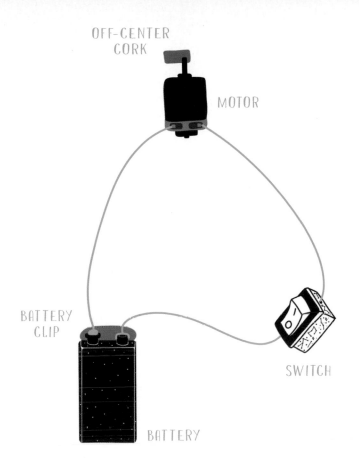

OFF-CENTER CORK

MOTOR

BATTERY CLIP

SWITCH

BATTERY

3. Imagine how you want your oracle-bot to look. There is no correct design and you can always go back and adjust features to experiment with how it moves. You will need some type of body on which to attach the circuit components, but you can also choose to add legs, a hole to view the words it wiggles over, or other features for pure aesthetics.

4. Hot glue the circuit components to the body. Switch it on to ensure the motor runs. It should not wiggle yet; don't worry.

5. Get an adult to help cut a ¼-inch slice of the cork, and poke a hole in it slightly off the center with the pen. You do not need to go all the way through the cork. Slip this over the shaft of the motor. It should be very snug.
6. If desired, decorate your oracle-bot.
7. Ask your first question, turn on the oracle-bot, and place it in the box to get your answer!

SCIENCE

While a motor is usually perfectly aligned so it does not shake, a lopsided cork is added here to create what's called an eccentric rotating mass motor. This applies uneven force to make the bot wiggle about to a random location. A cell phone uses a tiny eccentric motor to vibrate when you get a notification.

To extend this activity, you can attach markers or paintbrushes to the bot to have it create art after you're done with this project!

RUNE STONES

In these stones, we place our force.
They derive their power from that source.
Grouped together, grouped apart,
could it be the future they chart?

MAKE TRICK STONES THAT ATTRACT AND REPEL EACH OTHER LIKE MAGIC!

✧ Real rune stones are monoliths from the Viking Age with runes, the alphabet used by the Norse people who lived in Scandinavian lands and settlements around the North Atlantic, written on them. They often tell stories of war heroes and loved ones who had passed away.

✧ Some modern people who practice Wicca use small rune stones like these for divination or telling the future.

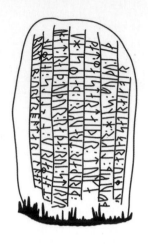

KARLEVI RUNESTONE

ᚠᚢᚦᚨᚱᚲ
ᚷᚹᚻᛏᛁᛋ
ᛈᛋᛃᛉᛏᛒ
ᛗᛖᛚᛜᛝᛟ

RUNES

SUPPLIES

+ Air-drying clay
+ Strong magnets
+ Something pointy to carve with
+ Paint

STEPS

1. Take a portion of air-drying clay, and form into an oval stone shape.

2. Press a magnet into each end, and cover with clay to conceal the magnets.

3. Carve a rune on each one, and set aside to dry according to the clay's instructions. Be sure not to put the stones too close so they don't attract each other while they're drying.
4. Paint the stones, and let dry.
5. Place the stones in a box, and gently shake the box, then turn it out on a table. Some of the stones will stick together. Use this to pretend to predict the future!

SCIENCE

Magnets have north and south poles due to how the atoms and their electrons are arranged. The north pole of one magnet will stick to the south pole of another, while two north poles will repel each other. The hidden magnets in the stones cause them to repel and attract each other, depending on what pole of the magnet is facing out. This would have looked very magical a long time ago, but you know the secret to how it works!

PLANET PORTAL

Energy stored, released to spin,
drop the colors that spread from within.
Earth and flora, their power unfurled,
together they create a hallowed new world.

MAKE A SPIN ART BOX TO CREATE YOUR OWN MULTIMEDIA PLANET-INSPIRED ART!

✧ Exoplanets are worlds outside our solar system. Using the spin art you create as a muse, try imaging how different some of these worlds may be.

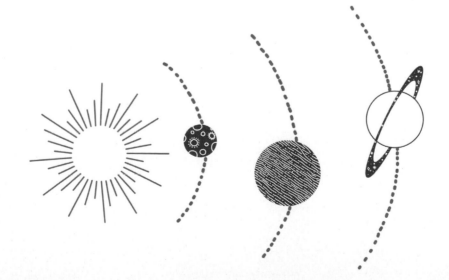

SUPPLIES

- ✦ Cardboard box
- ✦ Scissors
- ✦ 9 V battery clip with lead wires
- ✦ 9 V battery
- ✦ Hot glue
- ✦ Hobby motor
- ✦ Switch
- ✦ Paper
- ✦ Tape
- ✦ Paint
- ✦ Glue
- ✦ Items to make your planet, like dirt, sand, metal shavings, flower petals, glitter, etc.

STEPS

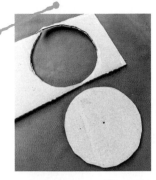

1. Cut the flaps off the cardboard box, and cut out the largest possible circle from one of the flaps. Poke a small hole through the center of the circle.

2. Take another flap, cut a 4-inch wide strip from it, and fold it in thirds. Cut a hole in the middle of the cardboard the same size as the motor base.

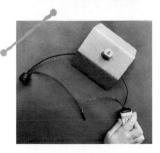

3. Attach the battery clip to the battery, and assemble the circuit according to the image to the left.

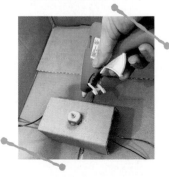

4. Hot glue the motor stand to the bottom center of the cardboard box. Slip the motor through the hole from under the stand, with the motor shaft facing up.

5. Affix the switch to the box with hot glue so it is easily accessible.

6. Add a dab of hot glue to the center hole of the cardboard circle from step one, and slide over the shaft of the motor. Hold in place till dry.

7. Turn on the switch. The motor should spin the cardboard circle. Turn it off.

8. Cut a circle from paper, and affix it to the spinning circle with tape.

9. Turn on the switch, and drip paint onto the spinning disc.

10. Pour glue onto the spinning art, and turn off the switch.

11. Apply the planet-making items to the glue design.

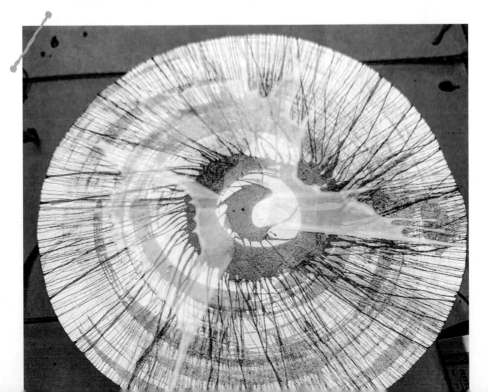

SCIENCE

When you drop paint onto the spinning paper, it appears as if it gets whisked off the page, away from the center of the circle. This is due to the centrifugal force, which is an outward force felt by something moving in a curved path. Centrifugal force is considered a fictitious force because it is the result of a combination of other forces in a system experienced only by the spinning item, but it is a very real force to that spinning item. It is responsible for squeezing out water from clothes in a washing machine, why our spinning Earth bulges at the equator, and how one day, we may have artificial gravity in space due to spinning spaceships. Try experimenting with your spin art box by using thinner or thicker paints, adding a lot or a little paint, or adding paint before or after you start the motor.

CHAOTIC CALLING

Pendulum swing, a predictable effect.
Invisible field—now the pendulum deflects.
Repeatable patterns, the dance is hypnotic.
Future can't be seen, the system is chaotic.

LEARN ABOUT CHAOS THEORY BY MAKING ART WITH MAGNETS AND A PENDULUM!

✧ Adult supervision recommended when handling strong magnets.

✧ If you don't have an outdoor space to do this, you can do a smaller scale version on a table-top using recycled items.

✧ Chaos theory describes cases where small changes in initial conditions have huge effects on the outcome. These appear as random and chaotic events to us, but patterns and similarities can be found within.

SUPPLiES

- ✦ Long stick
- ✦ Two things to hold the stick so it is parallel to and above the ground, like two chairs or sawhorses or tripods made from sticks
- ✦ Recycled plastic cup
- ✦ Scissors
- ✦ Tape or hot glue
- ✦ Strong magnets
- ✦ String
- ✦ Long piece of cardboard
- ✦ Two long pieces of paper
- ✦ Paint
- ✦ Water
- ✦ Glycerol (optional)

GLYCEROL

WATER

STEPS

1. Balance the stick on top of the tripods or chairs that you have set up back-to-back about three feet apart.

2. Poke a hole in the bottom of the plastic cup. Poke two holes across from each other near the top lip. The cup will hang from the string at these two holes.

3. Tape or hot-glue a strong magnet to the bottom of the cup.

4. Hang the cup from the stick with string so the cup is suspended close to the ground at its lowest point.

5. Put the cardboard under the stick and cup. Place one of the long pieces of paper over the cardboard.

6. Thin the paint with water and/or glycerol so it pours smoothly.

7. Add about ¼ cup of the paint mixture to the cup, plugging the hole at the bottom with your finger. Keeping the string taut, bring the cup up and out to about the edge of your paper, then let it go so it swings like a pendulum.

8. Vary the color of the paint and starting position of the cup, and see how it changes the paint design.

9. Place a new sheet of paper on the cardboard, then tape or hot-glue a few magnets under the paper near the center. Make sure the side of the magnets that is facing up is the one that will repel the magnet on the bottom of the cup. Repeat steps 7 and 8 to create a chaotic pendulum.

10. Repeat more runs of the chaotic pendulum, and compare the pieces of art.

SCiENCE

The force of gravity acting on the anchored cup drives the swinging motion of the pendulum. Friction with molecules in the air eventually slows it down, but the cup will follow a mathematically predictable path the whole time, even if you swing it spirally.

When you add magnets to the setup, they will repel the magnet on the cup and move it off course. Very slight changes in how the cup passes by the magnets will drastically change how the cup then dances around. You will never be able to repeat a pattern you create, no matter how exact you try to be. This is a demonstration of the mathematical concept of chaos. Chaos theory describes seemingly random and unpredictable events. Though the motion of your pendulum is predictable through mathematics, and its interaction with the magnets can also be described mathematically, the path it creates (evident in paint) still ends up being unpredictable because small changes in the initial drop of the pendulum have big impacts on the end result. Despite this, you can still see similarities and repeated patterns in the systems. These are hallmarks of chaos theory, which can be used to describe things like weather and fluid flow.

NORTH DIVINATION

Transfer the power to divine.
Guide the charges to form a line.
Leaf and water will reveal
the direction of the invisible field.

MAKE A HOMEMADE COMPASS!

✧ Flowing molten rock inside the Earth causes a circular flow of electricity that creates a large magnetic field around the Earth that extends into space. This field is what your compass will align with!

SUPPLIES

- ✦ Water
- ✦ Sewing needle
- ✦ Magnet
- ✦ Small leaf
- ✦ Compass or compass app (optional)

STEPS

1. Fill a small bowl with water.
2. Hold the needle by one end, and quickly slide the magnet from your fingertips to the other end in only one direction. Repeat this about 20 times.
3. Place the leaf on the water.
4. Place the needle on the leaf, and watch it turn.
5. Compare the direction the needle is pointing with the compass needle.

SCIENCE

The needle contains iron, but it is not magnetic. When you slide the magnet over the needle, it aligns the spin of the electrons in the needle and temporarily magnetizes it. This allows the needle to interact with the Earth's magnetic field. The interaction is weak, though, and the force of the friction of the needle on your finger or on the table is greater than the force from the magnetic field, so the needle will not react to it. When you place the needle on the leaf in water, it reduces friction enough that the needle can move and point north!

To extend this activity, make a treasure map where you need to use your homemade compass!

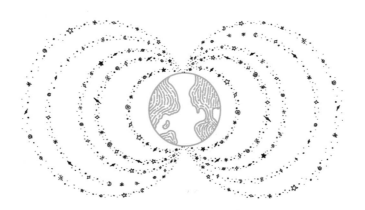

MAGNETIC MANIFESTATION

Current flows through the coiled course.

Domains align to exert their force.

One creates the other, the other creates one.

Remove an element, the effect is done.

GENERATE A MAGNETIC FIELD USING ELECTRICITY TO CREATE AN ELECTROMAGNET!

✧ Adult supervision required. The battery will get hot while making the electromagnet. Let it cool down if it starts to feel hot.

✧ Insulated wire must be used for this demonstration.

SUPPLiES

- ✦ Insulated copper wire, around 20–30 AWG
- ✦ Long iron nail
- ✦ Scissors, knife, or wire strippers
- ✦ Electrical tape
- ✦ 9 V battery
- ✦ 9 V battery clip with lead wires or alligator clips
- ✦ Small items that contain iron, such as paper clips, nails, or screws
- ✦ Switch

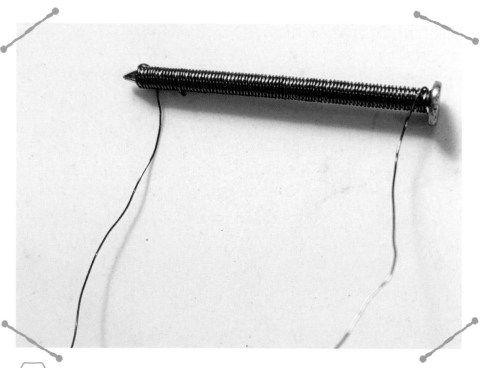

STEPS

1. Tightly wrap the insulated wire around the long nail as many times as possible in a single layer. Leave about two inches of wire at the beginning and end of the coil.

2. Expose the copper wire on either end of the coil. If using varnish-insulated wire, scrape away the varnish from the two ends of the wire using open scissors or a knife. The insulator is usually red. When scraped away, it should reveal the copper. If using plastic-coated wire, use wire strippers, scissors, or a knife to score the plastic about an inch from the ends and slowly remove the sheath.

3. Attach a battery clip lead to one side of the now-exposed coiled wire with electrical tape.

4. Attach the other side of the battery clip lead to the switch.

5. Attach the other side of the switch to the remaining side of the coiled wire. Ensure the switch is turned off.

6. Insert the battery into the battery clip.

7. Place the nail with the coiled wire into the pile of iron-containing items.

8. Turn on the switch and see the electromagnet turn on, attracting and picking up the items.

9. Turn off the switch and see the items fall.

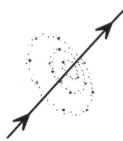

WHEN CURRENT PASSES THROUGH A CONDUCTOR, A MAGNETIC FIELD IS CREATED.

LOOPING THE WIRE INCREASES THE STRENGTH OF THE MAGNETIC FIELD.

SCiENCE

When we think of magnets, we commonly think of what are called permanent magnets—materials that always have a magnetic field capable of exerting a force, like a refrigerator magnet. It is possible, however, to *make* a magnetic field using electricity. When an electric current passes through a wire, a magnetic field is created. When certain wire is coiled, it increases the strength of the magnetic field. When a piece of soft iron, like a nail, is inserted into the coil, it further strengthens the magnetic field and small objects can be attracted using the current simply from an accessible at-home battery. Once the circuit is switched off, the electricity no longer passes through the coil and the magnetic field is lost.

Imagine what pure magic this effect must have seemed if demonstrated hundreds of years ago, before the relationship between electricity and magnetism was known. Even today electromagnetism can still amaze, but it is used behind the scenes in countless everyday items, including cars, refrigerators, speakers, and electric toothbrushes!

Under parental supervision, you can experiment with the electromagnet. How does changing the number of coils affect the strength of the magnet? What about using a different battery? Try using and comparing AAA, AA, C, and D alkaline batteries, which all have voltages of 1.5 but can deliver more current as they increase in size. How does increasing the current affect the strength of the electromagnet?

ALCHEMY

We can observe transformations all around us, like wood transforming to coal in a campfire or food scraps transforming to dirt in a compost pile. Chemists can transform compounds through chemical reactions. Some physicists can transform atoms in particle accelerators. This idea is not new, however. Hundreds of years ago, alchemists sought to blend magic and early scientific practices while attempting to change one substance into another.

TRANSMUTATIONS

Alchemists tried to create things like rejuvenating elixirs or cures for disease, but they are most known for attempting transmutations, or turning one element into another. Alchemists famously sought to turn common metals like lead into precious ones like gold. Though it is now thought that alchemists practiced more science than originally believed, their main fault was that many of their experiments were based on magic or superstition. They were not successful in many of their pursuits, but their ideas were not lost to the world.

In modern science, we have incredibly large devices called particle accelerators that can smash atoms together. This causes them to break apart and form other types of atoms, which is called nuclear transmutation. Though forming gold is not the goal of physicists, atoms of lead have been successfully smashed to form gold in particle accelerators, finally achieving the goal of alchemists. Though this transmutation process costs significantly more than the gold it creates, transforming other materials is more accessible than one might think! In this chapter, we will use the molecular treasures of the kitchen to perform some alchemy of our own.

PHYSICAL AND CHEMICAL CHANGES

We can divide transformations into two groups: chemical changes and physical changes. Chemical changes are when molecules react, breaking and creating new chemical bonds. This creates new substances that were not in the original mixture. Vinegar and baking soda reacting is an example of a chemical change—the molecules react to create new molecules like the carbon dioxide that creates the fizz. A physical change is when the molecule does not change but the state of its matter changes. Ice melting is an example of a physical change—the molecules of water do not change, but they transform from a solid state to a liquid state.

A common way to perform chemical reactions in the kitchen is by using microbes in a process called fermentation. Microbes were not discovered until the seventeenth century, but they have been used for millennia. From fungi leavening bread to bacteria transforming tea or milk, these everyday events were quite mysterious without the knowledge of these tiny creatures. We now know that fungi and bacteria can contain an assortment of enzymes, which are large biological molecules that can speed chemical reactions. For example, baker's yeast—the fungus used in bread making—can transform sugars into the carbon dioxide gas that allows the bread to rise.

We can also mix states of matter to create new materials through physical changes; these are called colloids. Foams are gas suspended in a liquid or solid, like meringue or whipped cream.

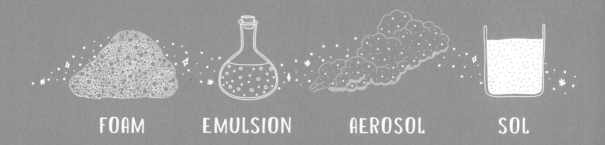

FOAM   EMULSION   AEROSOL   SOL

Emulsions contain a liquid suspended in another liquid, like milk or salad dressing.

Aerosols are liquids or solids suspended in gas, such as smoke or germs in tiny water droplets propelled through the air in a sneeze.

Sols or gels are solids suspended in a liquid, like paint or gelatin, respectively.

Can you identify the chemical and physical changes happening as you perform your kitchen alchemy in the following projects?

A FEW TYPES OF COLLOIDS

WHIPPED AQUAFABA

SALAD DRESSING

FOAM

A GAS SUSPENDED IN A LIQUID

EMULSION

A LIQUID SUSPENDED IN A LIQUID

SMOLDERING
WOOD SMOKE

CORNSTARCH
AND WATER

AEROSOL

A SOLID SUSPENDED
IN A GAS

SOL

A SOLID SUSPENDED
IN A LIQUID

STARCH TRANSMOGRIFICATION

Sun-captured carbon creates the chain
that forms the material we wish to attain.
Created by life, quickly ended by life,
things we create should not cause Earth strife.

CREATE A BIODEGRADABLE BIOPLASTIC FROM HOUSEHOLD ITEMS!

✧ Ask for an adult's help when using the stove.

✧ A polymer is a long molecule made with repeated units of a smaller molecule. A plastic is a material made from a moldable polymer. A bioplastic is a plastic made from renewable biological sources, preferably (but not always) ones that are biodegradable.

✧ Carbohydrates in plants are the products of photo-synthesis, the process by which plants store solar energy by capturing carbon dioxide from the air and forming energy-dense molecules from it. Starch, a long, branched chain of these molecules, is what the bioplastic will be made from.

SUPPLiES

- ✦ 2 tablespoons cornstarch
- ✦ ½ cup water
- ✦ 2 tablespoon vinegar
- ✦ 1–2 teaspoons glycerol/ glycerin
- ✦ Coloring (optional)
- ✦ Drying surface, like a recycled plastic container, stiff shiny leaf, wax paper, or a nonstick baking mat

STEPS

1. Mix the cornstarch, water, vinegar, and glycerol (and optional coloring) in a stove-safe pot.

2. Ask an adult to help heat the mixture over medium on the stove until it starts to boil, stirring constantly. Reduce heat to low, and stir until thickened and slightly translucent.

3. Thinly spread the mixture on your chosen drying surface, and let dry until stiff, about 2 to 3 days.

SCIENCE

The starch in cornstarch is tangled up in spherical globules. When you heat the starch in water, the individual starch polymers undergo a physical change and untangle. They interact with the water molecules, which thickens the mixture into a gel. The vinegar helps the starch untangle through a chemical change. As the mixture dries, water is removed, and the starch polymers get closer again but form a continuous sheet rather than globules, which creates the plastic. The glycerol makes the plastic more pliable, and the amount can be adjusted to get a more stiff or more bendable plastic. This recipe will create a thin, clear, flexible plastic. Experiment with the amounts of each ingredient to vary the properties of your plastic!

FORGE OF THE MICROBES

Harness the factories of the invisible world.
Chains of promise they will unfurl.
Harvest and process the gift they give
to create and use but then to outlive.

USE MICROBES IN KOMBUCHA TO GROW A BIOMAT, THEN DRY IT TO CREATE A LEATHER-LIKE MATERIAL!

✧ Adult supervision required. Ask an adult to help boil water.

✧ SCOBY stands for symbiotic culture of bacteria and yeast. Symbiotic means two organisms work together to benefit each other and themselves.

✧ The caffeine and sugar in the tea is used by the microbes, so don't use decaf tea or a sugar substitute.

SUPPLIES

- ✦ 8 cups water
- ✦ ½ cup white table sugar
- ✦ 4 bags black tea
- ✦ Unflavored, unpasteurized bottle of kombucha
- ✦ Clean, large widemouthed glass jar
- ✦ Clean cloth
- ✦ Rubber band
- ✦ Newspaper or cloth for drying
- ✦ Edible oil (coconut, canola, etc.)

STEPS

1. Bring the water to a boil on the stove in a covered pot.
2. Turn off the heat, add the sugar, and stir until dissolved.
3. Add the tea bags. Put the lid back on, and let the mixture cool to room temperature while the tea steeps.
4. Remove the tea bags, and add about half the bottle of kombucha. (You can drink the rest!)

5. Pour the inoculated tea into the large, wide-mouthed jar. Lay the cloth over the mouth of the jar, and secure with a rubber band.

6. Leave in a dark place at room temperature for about 4 weeks. Do not disturb it, but you can keep checking it. Eventually, a mat will develop on top of the tea. Wait until it is about a half a centimeter thick.

7. Remove the mat on top. This is called a SCOBY. Put the SCOBY between several sheets of newspaper or cloth, and put something heavy on top of it. Let dry for a few days.

8. Rub the dried SCOBY with a vegetable oil to make it more pliable.

9. To grow more mats, add fresh, cooled, sweetened tea from step 3 to ¼ of the leftover solution from step 7, and repeat step 6.

SCiENCE

Kombucha cultures contain many different species of bacteria and yeast, all of which participate to transform the sweetened tea into the kombucha. The microbes use the sugar and small molecules in the tea leaves to multiply and chemically change their surroundings—the tea. Some of these microbes have enzymes that can turn sugar into acetic acid, the acid in vinegar. This helps deter other microbes, like mold, from growing in the solution (but if you see mold on your SCOBY, throw it out and start over). Other microbes in the brew have enzymes that can create long chains of cellulose, which form the majority of the SCOBY. Cellulose is the same molecule that forms wood pulp and cotton. Many microbes can break down cellulose and use it as energy themselves, which makes the material from the SCOBY biodegradable!

AQUAFABA ASCENSION

Cicer arietinum provides the broth.
Furiously whipped, the concoction will froth.
More delicate than a butterfly's wing,
delectable charms it soon will bring.

USE THE LIQUID FROM A CAN OF CHICKPEAS (CALLED AQUAFABA) TO CREATE A STUNNING AND SWEET TREAT!

✧ The name aquafaba comes from the Latin words for water (aqua) and bean (faba).

CICER ARIETINUM

✧ A meringue is a dessert traditionally made using egg whites. It is hard on the outside, soft on the inside, and very delicate. The use of aquafaba to make a meringue was recently discovered by Joël Roessel, a French tenor, while experimenting in his kitchen.

◇ Liquid from other beans will not work as well as chickpeas/garbanzo beans. The liquid should be the consistency of egg whites. If not, add it to a pan and simmer until it thickens a little.

SUPPLIES

✦ Liquid from one (15-ounce) can unsalted chickpeas
✦ ¼ teaspoon cream of tartar (replace with lemon juice or vinegar if needed)
✦ ¼ cup superfine sugar
✦ Coloring, preferably powder (optional)
✦ Piping bag or spoon
✦ Nonstick baking sheet or parchment paper and baking sheet
✦ Toppings like lemon curd, chocolate mousse, berries, or edible flowers to decorate the meringue.

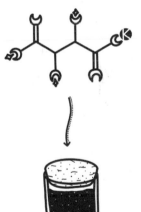

CREAM OF TARTAR

STEPS

1. Preheat the oven to 250°F.

2. Add the chickpea liquid to the bowl of a stand or hand mixer. Add the cream of tartar, and mix on high until soft peaks form.

3. Turn down the mixer to medium-low, and very slowly add the sugar. Add any coloring. Turn to high again, and whip until stiff peaks form.

4. Use a piping bag or spoon to gently spread the meringue into a 9-inch disk on the baking sheet.

5. Place in the oven, close the door, then turn the temperature down to 200°F. Bake for 1.5 to 2 hours until the meringue is firm on top. Turn off the oven, and allow it to cool before you take the meringue out. It's okay if it's overnight.

6. To serve, spoon your topping on top and decorate!

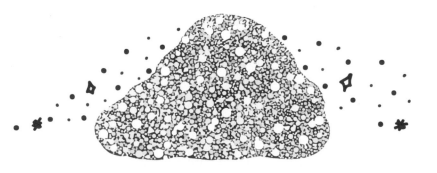

SCIENCE

A foam is a suspension of gas in a liquid or solid. The aquafaba contains molecules called saponins that are able to bridge the gas/liquid interface because they have one side that favors being in water (hydrophilic) and one side that favors being away from water (hydrophobic). When you whip the aquafaba, the saponins quickly organize their hydrophobic sides around the air, forming and trapping bubbles. They face their hydrophilic sides toward the water. Proteins in the aquafaba can participate in this too. Proteins are long chains folded into complicated three-dimensional structures, typically with hydrophobic parts of the chain on the inside of the structure and hydrophilic parts on the outside. The cream of tartar, which is an acid, helps unfold the proteins so the hydrophobic parts are exposed. This allows the proteins to also align at the gas/liquid interface and further support the foam formation. Baking solidifies this structure by removing the water, but it is still very fragile. This makes for an incredibly unique consistency for a food but also a challenge in the kitchen!

PRiMAL PiGMENTS

The vibrant gifts that our Earth bestows
will seep and let their colors flow.
At my hand, they will coalesce.
Create an image from this great finesse.

MAKE YOUR OWN WATERCOLORS AND PAINTS USING NATURAL PRODUCTS!

✧ Try items like coffee, beets, flower petals, paprika, cinnamon, turmeric, blueberries, or clay.

✧ Not everything is soluble in water, so don't worry if some items you try don't work. Write it down, and keep experimenting!

SUPPLIES

- Spices, vegetable or fruit juices, crushed petals, etc.
- Water
- Coffee filters
- Funnel
- Flour
- Paper
- Paintbrush

STEPS

1. Place chosen ingredients into small containers. Add a small amount of hot water to each sample if it isn't already a liquid. Crush larger things to release their inner juices. Let steep until the water is colored.

2. Filter the liquids from the solids using coffee filters and a funnel.

3. Use as is, as watercolors, or add a small amount of flour to each to get a thicker consistency.

4. Paint with your paints!

SCIENCE

Plants create many water-soluble pigments for uses such as pollinator attraction and chemical and pest protection. By steeping the colored plant parts in hot water, you are extracting the water-soluble pigments. Adding the flour creates a sol that thickens the paint and may help prevent clumping in some pigments.

Until fairly recently in human history, all paints and pigments were derived from plants, animals, or minerals. Many are still used today, such as carmine or cochineal, which are processed from insects and used in things like ink and cosmetics. Indigo is from a plant used to dye some brands of blue jeans.

MAGICAL MANNA

Tiny creatures consume then create
the gas that makes our fare inflate.
My charm has changed what is inside.
Break bread with me and find a surprise.

MAKE ARTISAN YEAST BREAD WITH A TWIST—A PURPLE CENTER!

✧ Ask an adult for help using the oven and knife.

YEAST

SUPPLiES

- ✦ 2 cups water
- ✦ 3–4 tablespoons dried butterfly pea flowers
- ✦ 1 tablespoon active dry yeast
- ✦ 1 tablespoon sugar
- ✦ 2 teaspoons salt
- ✦ 6 cups all-purpose flour, plus more for dusting
- ✦ Olive oil

STEPS

1. Boil the water. Remove from heat, and add the dried butterfly pea flowers. Steep for 10 minutes, then remove the flowers.

2. Pour the mixture into a large mixing bowl, and cool to about 110°F or slightly warm to the touch. Add the yeast and sugar. Stir to combine. Let stand for 5–10 minutes or until a foam forms on top. This

foam is the yeast creating carbon dioxide from sugar and oxygen!

3. Slowly add the flour and salt, stirring to combine.

4. Turn out the dough onto a work surface with a dusting of flour and knead for 5 to 7 minutes, until elastic and smooth.

5. Clean the mixing bowl, coat the inside with olive oil, and place the dough inside. Flip the dough to coat it with olive oil.

6. Place the bowl in a warm part of the house with a warm, damp kitchen towel over the top. Let rise for 2 hours.

7. Punch the dough down, remove from the bowl, and shape into two loaves.

8. Place the loaves on a greased baking sheet or baking stone, and slash the tops with a sharp or serrated knife. Let rise for 30 minutes.

9. Preheat the oven to 450°F. Bake the loaves for 10 minutes. Lower the temperature to 400°F, then bake for another 25 minutes.

10. Remove and cool on a cooling rack.

11. Slice with a serrated knife and reveal your colorful bread!

SCIENCE

Baking in general is all about chemistry and how different ingredients interact and react together. Yeast bread is especially interesting because you get to experience some microbiology in the kitchen too! Yeast is a fungus that consumes sugars and produces carbon dioxide. Kneading the dough rubs water and protein molecules in the flour together, creating somewhat of a mesh structure in the dough. This traps the carbon dioxide formed by the yeast and allows the bread to rise. An extra treat of this bread is the deep purple color of the interior. This is caused by heat-stable anthocyanins found in the butterfly pea flower!

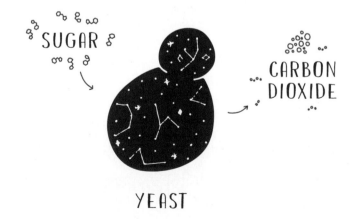

SUGAR

CARBON DIOXIDE

YEAST

SORCERER'S STONE

Peel away the flesh to reveal
an organic stone with magic concealed.
Fix and boil, the stone releases
pastel pinks to transform pieces.

EXTRACT PINK DYE FROM AVOCADO STONES!

✧ This type of extracted dye will only dye fabrics from plant or animal sources, like cotton, hemp, wool, or silk. It will not dye synthetic fabrics like polyester or nylon.

✧ Thoroughly wash the avocado stones (and skins, if using). Stones can be frozen while collecting enough to make a strong dye. Cleaned avocado skins can be dried and stored in an airtight container.

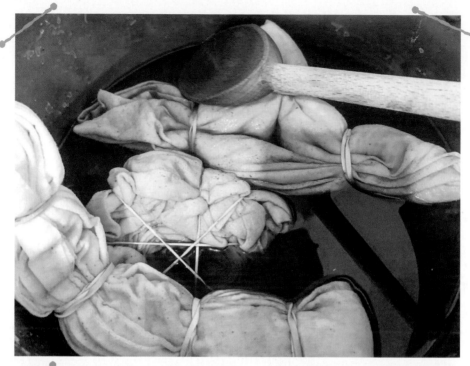

✧ Three avocado stones per large dish towel were used for these images.

SUPPLIES

* Fabric or yarn from a plant or animal source
* Alum
* Kitchen scale
* Clean avocado stones (skins may also be used but must be thoroughly cleaned of the green flesh), approximately enough weight to equal the weight of the fabric
* Baking soda
* Rubber bands or twine (optional)

STEPS

1. Add fabrics to a large stainless steel or enamel pot and add just enough water to cover the material.
2. Add a weight of alum equaling approximately the weight of the material.

3. Heat on the stove over medium heat, stirring to dissolve the alum.

4. Turn the heat to low and simmer for 1 hour, stirring frequently.

5. Remove the material from the pot and briefly rinse it in cold water, squeeze excess water, then set aside.

6. Discard the water in the pot, add the same amount of fresh water, and heat just to a simmer (do not boil).

7. Add the avocado stones.

8. Add a tablespoon of baking soda per four avocado stones. (This will make the dye a deeper pink, however the amount ultimately depends on the pH of your water. If your dye looks light pink or brown after a few hours, try adding more baking soda.)

9. Simmer on low for about 2 hours.

10. Meanwhile, fold and secure your fabric with rubber bands or twine to create tie-dye or shibori (a Japanese dyeing technique) designs.

11. Add the fabric to the pot and simmer for another 2 hours, stirring frequently.

12. Remove from heat.

13. Leave covered overnight or for two nights, depending on the desired intensity of color.

14. Rinse the tied fabric in the sink in cold water until the water runs clear, then undo the ties and rinse again.

15. Wash the fabrics with no other materials in the washing machine for the first wash. Then you may launder as usual.

SCiENCE

Dyeing fabrics with materials from nature is an age-old process. Though many natural products are highly pigmented, many are not suitable for use as a permanent dye as they do not readily become colorfast or they fade quickly due to time or sunlight exposure. For many natural dyes, something called a mordant must be used to bind the dye molecules to the fabric molecules. This was the purpose of the alum soak in the process above. Alum is a form of potassium aluminum sulfate. It gets sandwiched between the dye and fabric and holds the molecules together so the dye color will stay even after washing.

Synthetic fabrics were designed to have different properties than our commonly used naturally-derived fabrics, and therefore have very different molecular makeups. These synthetic materials are often hydrophobic, meaning they repel water. Dye molecules extracted in a water bath, like in the activity above, will be water soluble and hydrophilic (they like water) and therefore will not bind to the hydrophobic synthetic fabrics, even with a mordant. This is why synthetic fabrics cannot be used for this activity. Natural fabrics are generally hydrophilic, which make them a good match for hydrophilic dyes.

MiMiCRY

Nature has been a source of inspiration throughout history. Humans have tried to mimic the movement of birds through flight, the warmth of fur through clothing, and the diving ability of whales through the ballast of submarines. Designing technology after nature is called biomimicry. All forms of life on Earth discover solutions to challenges through a trial and error process called evolution. Scientists and engineers often look to nature for solutions to their own design problems, utilizing billions of years of evolution as inspiration. As we look closely at the spectrum of life on Earth to find this inspiration, we can notice many similarities. Perhaps the most enchanting of them all is the reoccurrence of the golden ratio.

THE GOLDEN RATIO

The golden ratio describes a specific relationship between certain objects' measurements. If a section is divided into two unequal parts, it follows the golden ratio if the ratio of the longer part to the shorter part is the same as the ratio of the whole section to the longer part. Examples of the golden ratio can be seen in snail shells, unfurling ferns, nautilus shells, leaf growth, and even animal horns. Seeing this pattern repeated throughout nature and the ability to relate it to mathematics gave this concept a divine aura to humans in history. People surmised that these equations could create the most pleasing and beautiful proportions.

This connection between numbers and nature stirred a mystical attraction to the shapes, and to this day, architects, musicians, and artists, along with mathematicians, scientists, and engineers, use this concept as inspiration. It is an enchanting story of connectedness but not the only example. Nature is an endless source of creative problem solving and also a beautiful muse. In this chapter, you will be creating art, like paintings, dances, and devices, by mimicking nature.

ARACHNID REVIVIFICATION

Weave a web to amuse and bewitch.
Conjure a spider controlled with a switch.
Help your creature keep the web taut,
but beware or you may get caught!

ASSEMBLE A WIGGLE-BOT THAT WILL SPIN A WEB WITH YOUR HELP!

SUPPLIES

+ Recycled plastic cup
+ Hobby motor
+ Hot glue
+ 9 V battery
+ 9 V battery clip with lead wires
+ Switch
+ Cork
+ Razor blade
+ String
+ Large piece of paper, different color than the string
+ Tape

STEPS

1. Poke a hole on one side of the cup near the bottom. This is where the string will leave the zombie spider.
2. Assemble the motor circuit according to the diagram.
3. Hot glue the circuit parts to the cup, being sure to balance the parts so the cup doesn't tip over.
4. With an adult's help, cut a ½-inch slice of the cork,

and poke a hole in it slightly off the center. Slip this over the shaft of the motor to create an eccentric rotating mass motor. Switch on the spider to ensure it wiggles.

5. Decorate your zombie spider.
6. Place a long length of string in the cup, and thread the end through the hole. Secure it to the paper with tape.
7. Turn on the zombie spider, and watch it dance around the page, creating a web. Help it anchor the web by taping the string as it goes.
8. Display the zombie spider art!

SCiENCE

Spiders have many amazing features that have inspired countless people. Scientists have tried to reproduce the properties of their strong yet flexible silk, and their webs have served as muses for everything from architecture to medicine. Though this project is a rudimentary interpretation of a spider, the contrast of a mindless, unskilled wiggle-bot to an elegantly evolved predator showcases the brilliance of the animal world.

FOREST NYMPH CONJURING

Arise from the Earth; stretch your fingers.
But only in the forest may you linger.
Your hand mirrors mine; you move as I do.
Back to the Earth, I bid you adieu.

CRAFT A MOVABLE HAND!

SUPPLIES

- Thin cardboard, like from a cereal box
- Pencil
- Scissors
- 14 short twigs of about the same size
- Hot glue
- Several long pieces of grass or flexible stems
- Slice of wood or something to create the palm

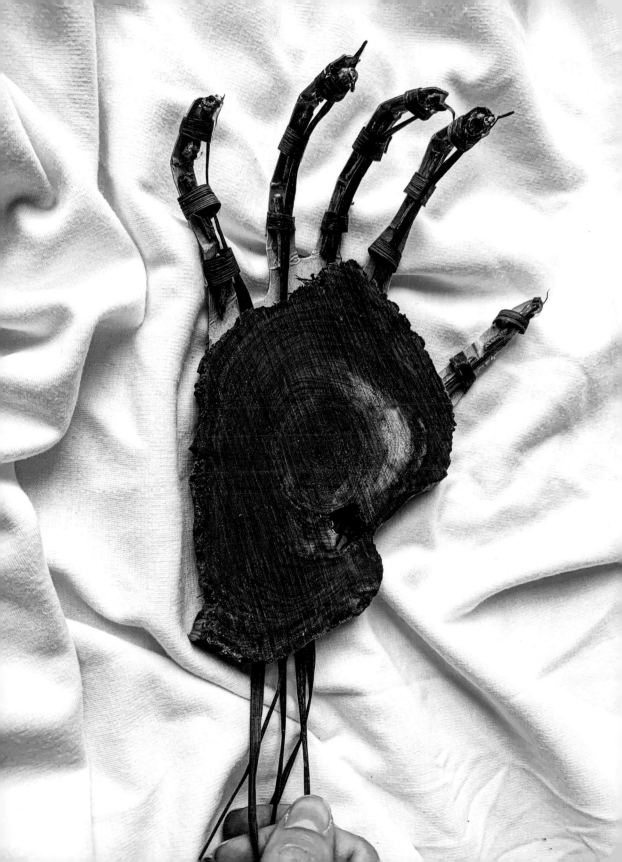

STEPS

1. Trace your hand on the cardboard, and cut it out.

2. Lay out the twigs as bones— three for each finger and two for the thumb, just like your own hand. Trim the twigs to size if needed, leaving about ¼ inch between each. Hot-glue them to the cardboard.

3. Trim the excess cardboard around the twigs. Crease the cardboard between each joint.

4. Hot-glue short pieces of grass, about 1 inch long, so that they form an arch over the middle of each twig.

5. Hot-glue a long piece of grass or stem at the tip of each digit, and thread it through each grass arch on that digit.

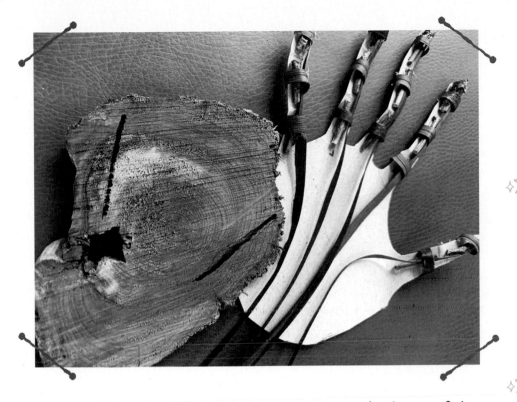

6. Gather the long grasses together at the base of the palm. Apply two thick, slanted strips of hot glue to the slice of wood so they guide the five strands of grass down to the base of the palm. Attach the wood to the cardboard gently, ensuring there is still enough room for the grasses to move freely under the wood.

7. Test out your forest nymph hand by gently pulling the grasses below the hand. They should move the fingers!

SCiENCE

This is actually very similar to how our own fingers move. Tendons are connected to the tips of our finger bones and stretch down to the base of the palm. These are called flexor tendons. They are threaded through tendon sheaths, just like the grass arches in the forest nymph hand, that hold the flexor tendon close to the bone to bend your fingers. This model is also mimicked in many robotic hands!

DANCE OF THE DRUIDS

Friend of all seasons, friend of mine,
speak to me through your dance divine.
Not a whisper needs to be spoken between,
Through glides and turns, our intent can be gleaned.

USE DANCE TO COMMUNICATE THE LOCATION OF A TREASURE!

✧ Not much is known about the Druids of over a thousand years ago, as they did not leave behind a written record, but more modern Druids celebrate nature and a respect for all living beings, most famously through dances around megaliths.

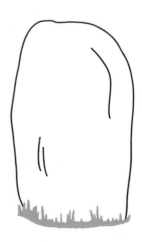

SUPPLIES

+ A friend
+ A treasure to hide
+ Paper and pencil

STEPS

1. Work with your friend to write down a set of dance moves that can describe movement around the yard or park. For example, a twirl to the right can be a signal to turn right, leaps can denote the number of steps, and a bow can signal that you have reached the treasure.

2. Begin from a marked starting point, keep track of your movements, and hide the treasure while your friend hides their eyes.

3. Translate the movements into dance, and see if they can find the treasure! Take turns being the dancer and seeker.

SCIENCE

Many members of the animal kingdom, in addition to humans, communicate through dance. One of the most amazing examples may be honeybees. Some biologists think bees use a complicated series of turns and wiggles, called the "waggle dance," to communicate the location of a patch of flowers in relation to the hive and the position of the sun!

Relating information through simple instructions is part of the basics of computer programming. All programs are based on a code—a series of steps followed by the computer to complete a task. By relaying the path to the treasure through coded dance, you are learning basic programming skills!

BIOMINERALIZATION

Add to the brew the chosen salt.
Its crystalline form we do exalt.
Atom by atom, the shape is decided.
The once organic now becomes hybrid.

GROW YOUR OWN BEAUTIFUL CRYSTALS!

✧ Ask an adult to help boil water.

SUPPLIES

+ Water
+ Epsom salts, borax, or alum
+ Item on which to grow crystals
  (feathers, dead insects, sticks,
  pine cones, etc.)

ALUM

EPSOM
SALT

BORAX

STEPS

1. Boil the water. Remove from heat, and pour into a heat-safe container. Use as little water as possible to cover your items; this will conserve your chosen salt.
2. Add your chosen salt slowly, stirring until no more will dissolve. The amount you add will vary based on how much water there is, which salt you use, and how hot the water is.
3. Add your items to the solution, or suspend your items with a string and pencil over the container (see drawing).

4. Set the container aside in a place where it won't be disturbed.
5. Check back on it periodically until no more crystal growth is seen.
6. Remove your items, and let dry.

SCiENCE

In this activity, you made a heated solution full of salt. A hot solution can dissolve more salt than a cool solution; this is called a supersaturated solution. When you cool the liquid down, salt begins to fall out of the solution, and if conditions are right, that salt can form crystals on things in the solution. Crystals form as atoms or molecules align in a repeated pattern. Different compounds and conditions can change this pattern and create differently shaped crystals.

Though inorganic crystals on organic materials may seem magical and peculiar, there are actually many examples of biological crystal growth in nature, called biomineralization. Familiar examples include our teeth and bones, which contain mineralized calcium phosphate, and shells, which are calcium carbonate. There are also more exotic examples, like magnetotactic bacteria that contain chains of small magnetic crystals. The bacteria use these magnets to align with the Earth's magnetic field like a compass needle!

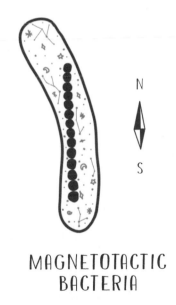

MAGNETOTACTIC
BACTERIA

MERCURIAL LARVA

Into the metal, its spirit is confined.
Freedom then restraint, the cell is designed.
Gravity pulls—a shift, a halt.
Weight is thrown; the larva vaults.

CREATE A TRICK TOY THAT FLIPS AND TURNS WHEN IT IS TILTED!

✧ Inertia: the tendency of an object to stay still or keep moving in the same direction until something else applies a force to it to change that movement.

SUPPLIES

- ✦ Aluminum foil
- ✦ 1 marble
- ✦ Shoebox lid

STEPS

1. Cut a piece of foil to about 4 inches by 3 inches.
2. Roll the foil around your finger or a marker to form a 4-inch tube so the marble just fits inside.
3. Put the marble inside, and gently fold closed one end of the tube around the curve of the marble, being sure not to crush the tube.
4. Roll the marble to the other end, and close it as above.
5. Place your device in the shoebox lid, and tilt the lid. The mercurial larva should tip and turn on its own with just the slightest tilt.

SCIENCE

As you tilt the box, the marble rolls to the other end of the tube and hits the closed end. Since the foil is light and curved, the marble has enough inertia to keep rolling, but it causes the empty part of the tube to roll upward then down in the direction the marble was traveling. Now the marble is free to roll to the other side, and the process repeats, making it look like the toy has a mind of its own!

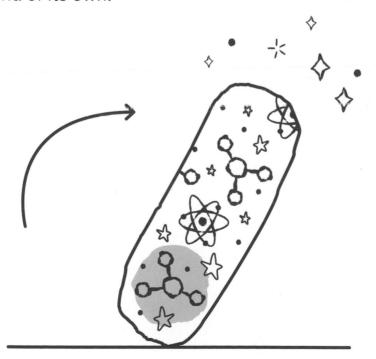

BEWITCHING BLOSSOMS

Spread through the water, up through the cutting.
Carried through stem, the compound is flooding.
Unseen till illuminated with UV
observe the path and see like a bee.

MAKE FLUORESCENT CUT FLOWERS!

✧ Protect your work surface and hands. The highlighter may stain.

✧ Some flowers have fluorescent features already on them. For fun, be sure to inspect your flowers under a black light before you begin the activity to see if yours have any! Since many pollinators can see UV light, scientists think these decorations on the flowers serve to attract pollinators.

SUPPLIES

- ✦ Yellow highlighter
- ✦ Pliers
- ✦ Small clear vase
- ✦ White cut flowers, such as daisies, roses, or carnations
- ✦ Scissors
- ✦ Black light

STEPS

1. Open the highlighter casing with pliers to get to the ink cartridge inside. You can usually pull out a cap on the non-writing end to access it.

2. Fill the vase about halfway with water and dunk the highlighter cartridge in it. Squeeze the cartridge until the water is dyed bright yellow.

3. Cut the bottom inch of the flowers' stems off at an angle with the scissors. Remove any lower leaves that will be submerged in water.

4. Add the flowers to the vase and wait anywhere between an hour and a few days.

5. Shine the black light on the flowers every now and then to see the progress of the highlighter dye being taken up by the flowers. Take pictures before, during, and after under the black light to compare the dye uptake.

SCiENCE

Yellow highlighters contain the molecule fluorescein, which is highly a fluorescent compound. Fluorescence is the phenomenon that occurs when a molecule can absorb one type of light, and then send out a different type of light. Since the black light has high energy photons that we cannot see, when the fluorescein fluoresces under a black light, it looks like the light is being created from nothing!

When the flowers are placed in the vase, the fluorescein solution is taken up through the stem and into the flowers through a process called transpiration. Water molecules (carrying other molecules in the solution) fight gravity and travel up the stem in thin tubes called xylem using capillary action. Capillary action involves water molecules being attracted to the sides of the xylem, called adhesion, and also to each other, called cohesion. The net result is the water moving upwards, flowing into cells in the leaves and flowers. As water evaporates from the leaves, this creates room for more water to enter the top of the plant, further contributing to the transport of water upwards.

GLOSSARY

Anthocyanin: A type of molecule found in many plants as a pigment. It can be used as a pH indicator as its color can change as the pH changes.

Atom: An incredibly small unit of matter that makes up the world around us. They are made of a central nucleus containing protons and neutrons surrounded by a cloud of electrons.

Bacteria: Small single-celled organisms. There are countless numbers of bacteria on Earth.

Battery: A device that can store energy as chemical energy then convert it to electrical energy when part of a circuit.

Biomineralization: The ability of some lifeforms to create inorganic structures. Examples include teeth, bones, and seashells.

Charge: A characteristic of some types of matter that describes how it will be affected by magnetic or electric fields.

Compound: A substance that is made of one type of molecule that was created by the bonding of at least two different types of atoms.

Conductor: A material that allows electricity to flow through it.

Crystal: A structure made of matter arranged in a repeating pattern.

Dissolve: When a substance enters a liquid, separates into smaller parts, and becomes surrounded by the molecules of that liquid.

Electron: A negatively charged particle that exists in a cloud-like space around atoms. It is also the carrier of electricity in circuits.

Electron spin: Electrons have a property that can be described as "spinning"; however it is more complicated than simply spinning. The direction of the spin gives rise to phenomena such as magnetism.

Energy: The ability to do work.

Enzymes: Large, complicated molecules found in lifeforms that perform a task, like making or breaking a molecule.

Evaporate: The process of a liquid turning into a gas or vapor.

Fermentation: The process of microorganisms, like fungus or bacteria, breaking down molecules to create other molecules through the action of enzymes.

Field: An area in which a force can be felt or detected. For example, a magnetic field is the area around a magnet that the force of magnetism affects.

Fluorescence: A phenomenon where a material absorbs light of a certain energy, then releases light of a lesser energy.

FLUORESCENCE

Force: An effect that can change the motion of an object.

Friction: The force resulting when one surface rubs over another surface. This is brought about by a slight attraction between molecules on the two surfaces. These add up to resist the movement of the whole.

Fungus: A type of organism that ranges from unicellular organisms like yeast to multicellular ones like mushrooms.

Hydrophilic: Referring to a substance that is attracted to water, meaning "water loving."

Hydrophobic: Referring to a substance that repels water, meaning "water fearing."

Indicator: A substance that changes color due to a certain pH change.

Inertia: A tendency of an object to remain at rest or remain in motion unless acted on by a force.

Inoculate: To introduce microbes or cells into a growth medium.

Inorganic: Referring to a substance that does not contain carbon.

LED: Short for "light emitting diode," contains certain semiconductor materials that create light when part of a circuit.

Microbe: A name for a microscopic organism, such as bacteria or fungi that are so small that they must be viewed with a microscope.

Molecule: Atoms bonded together in a certain shape to make the basic unit of many substances.

Motor (electric): A machine that converts electrical energy to kinetic energy.

Nuclear fusion: A reaction in which the nuclei of atoms are joined to form a new nucleus. This reaction releases a great deal of energy.

Nucleus (physics): The center of an atom containing the sub-atomic particles, protons, and neutrons.

Organic: Referring to a substance that contains carbon and that is from a biological source.

pH: A scale of 0–14 describing the acidity or basicity of a solution. Lower numbers are more acidic while higher numbers are more basic. A value of 7 is neutral.

Pharmaceutical: A compound that has been scientifically shown to treat a disease or condition, also known as a drug.

Pigment: A substance that is deeply colored.

Pollinator: An animal that assists plants in transferring pollen between their reproductive organs.

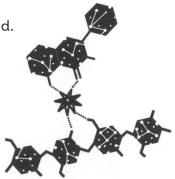

Polymer: A molecule made of repeating units attached together.

Reaction: When one or more substances are transformed into one or more different substances. A chemical reaction is when molecules react. A nuclear reaction is when atomic nuclei react.

Salt: A compound made of two substances that are oppositely charged, called ions.

Soluble: Able to be dissolved or taken up by a solution.

Solution: A liquid with one or more dissolved compounds within it.

Tendon: A strong fiber that attaches bone to muscle.

Transmute: To change the type of an atom, called an element, to another.

VISIBLE   ULTRAVIOLET

UV light: Short for ultraviolet light, a form of electromagnetic radiation that has higher energy than visible violet light. Human eyes cannot see UV light.

Wax: A hydrophobic substance that is a moldable solid at room temperature.